Collins
English for Life

B2+ Upper Intermediate

Speaking

Nicola Prentis

Collins

An imprint of HarperCollins Publishers
Westerhill Road
Bishopbriggs
Glasgow
G64 2QT

HarperCollins Publishers
Macken House
39/40 Mayor Street Upper
Dublin 1
D01 C9W8

First edition 2014

10

© HarperCollins Publishers 2014

ISBN 978-0-00-754269-7

Collins® is a registered trademark of HarperCollins Publishers Limited

collins.co.uk/elt

A catalogue record for this book is available from the British Library

Typeset in India by Aptara

Printed by Ashford Colour Press Ltd

This book contains FSC™ certified paper and other controlled sources to ensure responsible forest management.

For more information visit: www.harpercollins.co.uk/green

About the author

After six years teaching in Europe, Australia and Asia, **Nicola Prentis** did an MA in ELT in York, England. Nicola then continued teaching abroad but took a new interest in designing materials. In 2010, she started writing graded readers and contributed to coursebooks and digital content for various publishers. She finds it difficult to stay in one place and has lived in 12 cities in 12 years. At present she's happily living in Madrid but is very tempted by Burlington, Vermont, USA.

CONTENTS

INTRODUCTION

English for Life: Speaking B2+ will improve your spoken English in a variety of everyday situations and contexts.

You can use *Speaking B2+* in the classroom as supplementary material for a general English course, or it is also suitable for self-study.

Speaking B2+ will help you develop your communication skills in different areas, including:

- showing tact, interest, confidence, support, excitement, annoyance, scepticism and sarcasm
- handling negotiations, awkward conversations and communication problems
- exchanging complex information
- admitting and denying things
- persuading people
- making yourself heard
- talking about money, complaining about a bad day, and sharing gossip

Speaking B2+ comprises a **book** and **online audio**. The book has 20 units. At the back of the book there is:

- an appendix expanding on the *Everyday language* phrases from the units, offering examples of real-life usage taken from the Collins COBUILD Corpus
- a mini-dictionary taken from Collins COBUILD Advanced Dictionary
- a comprehensive answer key
- a full transcript of the audio material

The online audio contains a wide variety of realistic audio conversations, plus plenty of speaking practice activities. You can download the audio at **collins.co.uk/eltresources**.

Using *Speaking B2+*

You can either work through the book from Unit 1 to Unit 20, or you can pick and choose the units that are most useful to you. The contents page will help you in your selection of units and your own plan for learning.

For ease of use, each of the 20 units follows the same format. It is recommended that you follow the order of exercises when working through a unit. Each unit includes the following sections:

Conversations – listen to and read 3–4 conversations. Key words and phrases are presented in bold.

Understanding – check your understanding of the conversations.

Saying it accurately – focus on using the right words and phrases.

Saying it appropriately – focus on tone and on using language that is appropriate to the context.

Get speaking – an opportunity to practise speaking. Often this involves interacting with a speaker when using the online audio in a role-play.

Everyday language – a set of phrases that are useful everyday phrases not necessarily related to the theme of the unit.

Next steps – a practical way to find out further information about the topic of the unit or a tip on how to use the language in real life.

There are also **Language notes, Cultural notes** and **Speaking tips** in several of the units.

Study tips

- Each unit should take about 60–75 minutes to work through. Take regular breaks and do not try to study for too long. 30 minutes is a good length for an independent learning session.
- Revise and go over what you have learned regularly.
- Put the audio tracks on your mobile phone so you can listen to the conversations and practice activities on your way to work or when you're out jogging or walking.
- Try to find someone with whom you can practise your English, either face-to-face, over the phone or online.
- Note down the language you find most useful and develop a system for recording it in a useful way. Try to learn a maximum of two or three new phrases or items a day.
- Test yourself using the *Get speaking* sections.

Other titles

Also available in the *Collins English for Life* series at B2+ level: *Listening, Reading* and *Writing*.

Available in the *Collins English for Life* series at A2 level and B1+ level: *Speaking, Listening, Reading* and *Writing*.

Using the online audio

 This icon indicates that there is an audio track that you should listen to. Please note that the audio is available to download for free from **collins.co.uk/eltresources**.

---

1 BUMPING INTO PEOPLE

Getting started

1 If you meet an acquaintance unexpectedly, what kinds of things do you talk about?

2 Is it different if you bump into an old friend? What do you talk about then?

Conversations

  Read and listen to extracts from three conversations. How well do you think the speakers know each other?

01

Conversation 1

Beth: Hi John, **fancy seeing you here!**

John: Beth, hi! **Long time, no see!**

Beth: Yeah, not since George's wedding, I think. **How have you been?**

John: Good, good. How about you? You were in the middle of buying a house, weren't you? **How did that go?**

Beth: Don't remind me! It was a nightmare.

John: Rather you than me. I'm sticking to renting.

Beth: Don't blame you. I never want to buy a house again! But anyway, what about you?

John: **Oh, no major news really.**

Beth: Hey, **we should go for a coffee sometime**, catch up properly.

John: **Definitely. Give me a ring** and we'll work something out. You've got my number, haven't you?

Conversation 2

Mary: Hi! **How are you?**

Conor: Tired. I ended up staying at the party till really late last night. **How are you?**

Mary: Yeah, I'm glad I left early. **What are you up to?**

Conor: Just sorting out a few things.

Mary: **Do you fancy** getting some lunch?

Conor: **Sorry, can't stop.** I'm in a bit of a rush, actually.

Mary: Oh? **Where are you off to?**

Conor:	I'm on my way to Laura's for lunch. And she's expecting me at one.
Mary:	**You'd better get off then**. I know what she's like, and I'd hate to be in your shoes if you're late!

Conversation 3

Karl:	Hi! **It's** Yana, **isn't it?**
Yana:	Yeah, hi, er …?
Karl:	Karl. We met at that sales conference last month.
Yana:	Oh yes, right. Sorry.
Karl:	How's work?
Yana:	You know, **same old same old.**
Karl:	I heard your firm won that big new banking client. I hope they're handing out promotions!
Yana:	Yeah, let's hope so. **Listen, nice to see you again** but **I'd better be off.** My friend'll be wondering where I've got to.
Karl:	Sure.
Yana:	Bye!
Karl:	**See you around.**

Understanding

1 Write the correct conversation number for each description below.

1 A conversation between people that don't know each other well: ....

2 A conversation between people that know each other well but don't see each other often: ....

3 A conversation between people that see each other often: ....

2 Look at the bold phrases in Conversations 1–3 and match them to the strategies a–e below.

a Asking/checking someone's name

b Catching up with news and making small talk

c Inviting someone

d Responding to an invitation

e Ending the conversation

3 Answer the questions.

1 In Conversation 1, Beth suggests they go for a coffee 'sometime'. Why do you think she doesn't try to make a definite arrangement?

2 In Conversation 2, why doesn't Mary answer when Conor asks 'How are you?'?

3 In Conversation 3, why do you think Yana doesn't ask Karl directly what his name is?

Saying it accurately

1 Complete the sentences with the words and phrases from the box.

time no see	fancy seeing you	major news	get off then
are you off to	terrible with	fancy going for	
can't stop	better be off	are you up to	

1 Oh, I'm .... names, sorry, uh … ?

2 Anyway, I'd .... or I won't get to the bank before it closes.

3 I don't often see you in town. What .... ?

4 Do you .... a coffee?

5 Sorry, I .... I'm really busy today.

6 Where .... ?

7 You'd better .... You don't want to be late!

8 Nick! Hey, ... here!

9 Sue Johnson! Long .... !

10 I'm fine. No .... , really. I'm still doing the same job.

Saying it appropriately

1 Listen to Beth in Conversation 1. Underline the word Beth stresses. Why does she stress that word?

2 Now listen to two different versions of the questions below. How does it change the meaning if the stress is different?

1 How are <u>you</u>?
How <u>are</u> you?

2 How have you been?
How have you <u>been</u>?

3 Listen again and repeat the questions.

4 In English, intonation is used to show interest. Listen to six short conversations. How does the second speaker in each conversation sound?

1	a annoyed	**b** happy		**c** confused
2	a sincere	**b** annoyed		**c** confused
3	a happy	**b** annoyed		**c** sincere
4	a uninterested	**b** angry		**c** happy
5	a happy	**b** depressed		**c** annoyed
6	a depressed	**b** impatient		**c** interested

5 Listen to these responses. Repeat the sentences, copying the intonation.

1 Yeah, right. Another time then. See you around!

2 Hi! Sorry, I'm terrible with names … Er …

3 Stressed! Work's crazy! How are you?

Get speaking

1 Read the situations and think about what you might say in the conversations below. Then play the audio. Listen and respond when you hear the beeps.

1 You bump into an old friend in the street. He starts the conversation.
- Respond and ask how he is.
- Respond with your news.
- Accept the invitation or make an excuse.

2 You bump into someone you don't know well.
- Ask her name.
- Tell her some different news.
- Bring the conversation to an end.

Language note

The phrases highlighted in this 'Everyday language' section of every unit are particularly useful because you can change the words and use them in many different situations. They take the form ***The problem with X is Y***.

***The problem with** winter **is** the cold.*

***The problem with** starting your own business **is** getting a loan from the bank.*

***The problem with** you **is** you're too sensitive.*

Everyday language

Match the phrases 1–5 from the conversations to their meanings a–e.

1 You were in the middle of
2 I'd hate to be in your shoes if
3 I'm sticking to
4 Rather you than me!
5 Don't blame you.

a I wouldn't like to be you if … happens.
b I'm glad I'm not doing that!
c I'll carry on with
d I can understand why you'd feel that way.
e You were busy doing

These phrases are your Everyday language phrases for this unit. Go to page 88 to see these phrases in context. Then try to use them yourself.

Next steps

Learn one phrase every day and then try to use it as soon as you can. Write it on a sticky note and put it on the mirror when you're brushing your teeth so you see it often!

2 TALKING ABOUT YOURSELF

Getting started

1   In what situations do you talk about yourself?
2   What kind of things do you tell people about yourself in those situations?

Conversations

07

1   Read and listen to extracts from three conversations.

Conversation 1

Interviewer:	So, why do you think you're suited to this job?
Lucy:	Well, I've just done an MA in Journalism, so the fact that **I've got a background in** both fashion and journalism means that I'm able to see fashion writing from all angles.
Interviewer:	What would you say your strengths are as a writer?
Lucy:	**I work well in high pressure situations** and **I've been told that I'm particularly good at** coming up with good ideas for articles.
Interviewer:	How do you deal with criticism? For example, if an editor wants you to redo an article.
Lucy:	Generally, **when I've been in that situation in the past, I've** always found it's good to remember that it's not personal and then find out exactly what they want me to change.
Interviewer:	Could you tell me about a time when you had to deal with a tight deadline?
Lucy:	**I take a lot of pride in** beating deadlines, like last month I had to write a series of pieces …

Conversation 2

Jameela:	**I'm hopeless at** filling in these online profile things. What do you think I should put for this: *How would your best friend describe you?*
Sally:	Easy. You're outgoing, easy to talk to, a good listener. How many things do you need to put?
Jameela:	Yeah, but **I'm not the kind of person who** can just start a conversation with anyone. Like at parties where I don't know people. I'm actually quite shy.

Sally:	You? Shy? You must be joking!
Jameela:	I am! Underneath it all I'm not that confident.
Sally:	Well, you hide it well. You're much better than me at networking. That **isn't really my strong point.**
Jameela:	But you do it for your job all the time!
Sally:	Yeah, but that's different, isn't it? I don't have a choice then. It's my job. **I wouldn't say that I** make friends easily in real life. I **tend to** stick with my old friends and not mix outside that group.

Conversation 3

Will:	What are you wearing that for?
Roman:	I'm going to my karate class.
Will:	Since when do you do karate?
Roman:	I only started it a couple of months ago but **I'm really into** it now.
Will:	Should I be scared of you now, then?
Roman:	Yeah, you'll think twice about stealing my milk out of the fridge when I'm a black belt!
Will:	Good that you're doing something though. **I'm a bit of a** couch potato really.
Roman:	I noticed!
Will:	Hey!
Roman:	Seriously though, it's not just about fitness, it's a whole mind–body thing. **I can't get enough of it,** and you might like it more than you think. Come along one week and try.
Will:	Okay, next week maybe.

Language note

In a conversation people often respond with very short chunks instead of full sentences. In Conversations 2 and 3 there are lots of these chunks:

Easy. *I noticed!*

You? Shy? *Okay, next week maybe.*

Understanding

1 Look at the bold phrases in Conversations 1–3. Match them to strategies a–e below.

a Talking about your strengths **d** Talking about your experience

b Talking about your weaknesses **e** Talking about things you like

c Talking about yourself in general

Saying it accurately

1 Complete the sentences with the words and phrases from the box.

told that	that situation	background in	strong point
tend	kind of person who	high pressure	lot of pride

1 I'm not the .... you'd expect to be into finance but I've been following international stock markets since I was a teenager.

2 I've got a .... accounting which means that I understand the main accountancy software systems.

3 I've been .... I'm particularly good at managing people.

4 I take a .... in my ability to get on with all sorts of different people.

5 I work well in .... situations so I manage deadlines very well.

6 When I've been in .... in the past, I've always focused on making people see that I'm taking their problem seriously.

7 I .... to go for sales-based jobs because I like the excitement of that kind of environment. Time management isn't my .... unfortunately.

2 Match the sentences in Exercise 1 to the interview questions a–e below. Sometimes more than one answer is possible.

a What would you say are your weaknesses? ....

b How do you think your experience will help you in this job? ....

c What do you see as your strengths? ....

d Tell me a little bit about yourself. ....

e Tell me about a time when you had to deal with a difficult customer. ....

3 Complete the conversation with the correct phrases. Use the words in brackets and add any other necessary words.

Inna: I'm really nervous about giving this seminar tomorrow. I'm sure I'm going to forget everything.

George: Of course you won't! You're the **1** ......*kind of person*...... (kind) who remembers everything.

Inna: This is different. I hate speaking in public.

George: I used to go to a university society that practises public speaking. I used to be terrified of it too but now I'm **2** .... (into). You should try it.

Inna: Do you think it'll work? I **3** .... (tend) be better at things once I've done them a few times.

George: Yeah! Once you start giving seminars, you won't be able to **4** .... (enough)!

Saying it appropriately

1 Read and listen to extracts from four interviews. Mark the places where the interviewees pause. Which interviewees use pauses for emphasis? Why do the other interviewees pause? Which people use stress to sound confident?

1 **Interviewer:** What do you consider to be your strengths?
Mick: Well, I think I'd say that most people find me to be a good leader.

2 **Interviewer:** What do you consider to be your strengths?
Stefan: Well, I think I'd say that most people find me to be a good leader.

3 **Interviewer:** Tell me about your most recent sales job.
Laura: My most recent job in sales was very similar to the position your company is offering.

4 **Interviewer:** Tell me about your most recent sales job.
Mika: My most recent job in sales was very similar to the position your company is offering.

2 Listen to the interviewees in extracts 2 and 4 again. Repeat their answers, copying their stress and using pauses to help you sound confident.

Get speaking

1 Read the situations and think about what you might say in the conversations below. Then play the audio. Listen and respond when you hear the beeps.

1 You are in a job interview.
- Talk about yourself. Relate it to your work.
- Talk about your experience and make it relevant to the job.
- Talk about your strengths in relation to the position.
- Talk about your weaknesses but try to turn them into something positive about yourself.
- Describe a difficult situation you have been in and what you did to resolve it.

Everyday language

1 Look at Conversations 2–3 on pages 12–13 again. Find phrases with the meanings below.

Conversation 2

This is difficult to believe.

The reality is I'm not the way I appear to be.

Conversation 3

I didn't know you did that!

You won't want to do this!

I want to stop joking now.

The answers to the exercise above are your Everyday language phrases for this unit. Go to page 88 to see these phrases in context. Then try to use them yourself.

Next steps

The interview questions in this unit are based on real interviews. Practise answering them for a job you would like to do. Record and listen to your answers, noting any hesitations or repetitions, then try again.

3 TELEPHONE AND COMMUNICATION PROBLEMS

Getting started

1 Do you often speak in English on the phone or the Internet?
2 What kinds of problems and breakdowns in communication can happen?
3 What other situations can be difficult to communicate in?

Conversations

10

1 Read and listen to extracts from four conversations.

Conversation 1

Rosa: Hi, Dad! Can you hear me? Can you hear me? I'm ...

Dad: Hi, Rosa!

Rosa: Oh, good. You're there. Dad? How are you?

Dad: Yes, I can hear you.

Rosa: Hey, Dad, I'm **getting a delay**, so I'm ...

Dad: Yes, yes I'm here. I'm fine, thanks. How are ...?

Rosa: Dad, I'm going to hang up and try calling you back, Okay?

Dad: Okay, love.

Rosa: Hi, is that better this time?

Dad: Loud and clear.

Rosa: I was just calling to ask about summer. Are you still coming over?

Dad: We just booked the flights for Ma-ma-ma-may-y-y-y - fif-fif-fif- ...

Rosa: **I didn't get most of what you just said.** Did you say May? ... **You're breaking up.** This is useless.

Conversation 2

Dave: ... the hotel is The Mand ... on De Souza Street.

Kat: The where? **You keep coming and going,** this connection's awful.

Dave: It's fine at my end. I'll type that bit. Did you get it?

Kat: Sorry **my connection went** completely ... . Oh, your message just came through too. Great, thanks.

Conversation 3

Vanya:	Hello.
Terry:	Hi!
Vanya:	Hello?
Terry:	Hi, Vanya, it's me. Are you there?
Vanya:	Terry? I can't hear you. Can you hear me?
Terry:	I can hear you. Can you hear me now? Hello?
Vanya:	Hi, I don't know why **we got cut off.**
Terry:	Yeah, sorry, **the reception here's terrible.** I had to come out to the car park to get a better signal.
Vanya:	Where are you?
Terry:	I'm at the conference. Where are you?
Vanya:	Still stuck on the train. And **my battery's low** so I can't talk long.
Terry:	How long do you think you'll be?
Vanya:	Another half an hour. Meet me at the …
Terry:	Hello? Oh …!

Conversation 4

Announcer:	… Area 4 … o'clock …
Pilar:	**What are they saying?**
Neil:	Shhh, let me listen.
Announcer:	… tent … works …
Pilar:	**I didn't hear a word of that!**
Neil:	I think they said the jazz is somewhere else but **I didn't catch** where. Wait!
Announcer:	… jazz … main tent …
Pilar:	What? **Did you get that?**
Neil:	Yep. It's in the main tent. Let's go!

Language note

When you find yourself in a situation where you can't make out what someone is saying, whether it's because of technical issues, an unfamiliar accent or for any other reason, you will often have to repeat several times that you haven't understood them. For this reason, it's worthwhile memorizing a few different ways to ask someone to repeat what they said. This will allow you to confidently deal with the difficulty at hand, without having to worry about your language *as well as* the communication issue.

Understanding

1 Look at the bold phrases in Conversations 1–4 and write them under the correct headings in the table.

Describing a problem with technology	Saying you didn't hear what someone said	Asking someone else if they heard something
1	1	1 ....
2	....	2 ....
3	2	
4	3	
5		
6		
7		

Saying it accurately

1 Complete the sentences with the words from the box. You won't need two of the words.

1 I'm .... a delay.
2 You're .... up.
3 You keep .... and ....
4 My battery's .... so I can't talk long.
5 We got .... off.
6 My connection ....
7 What are they .... ?

saying	low
having	cut
losing	getting
went	going
coming	breaking

2 Cross out the verb that cannot be used to complete these phrases.

1 I didn't *get / hold / catch / hear* most of what you just said.
2 Did you *get / catch / have / hear* that?

Saying it appropriately

1 Listen to the sentences below. Notice the weak forms (grey text) and where the words run together (underlined).

1 Sorry, I didn't hear you. You're breaking up.
2 Say that again. You keep coming and going.
3 Sorry about that – we got cut off.
4 I didn't get most of what you just said then.
5 I didn't catch a word of that!

2 Listen again and repeat the phrases. Copy the weak forms and the way some words run together.

 3 Listen to extracts from nine conversations. Choose the most appropriate thing to say next.

12

1	**a**	You're breaking up.	**b**	I'm getting a delay.
2	**a**	We got cut off.	**b**	You keep coming and going.
3	**a**	What are they saying?	**b**	I didn't get most of what you just said.
4	**a**	I'm getting a delay.	**b**	The reception here's terrible.
5	**a**	They keep coming and going.	**b**	What are they saying?
6	**a**	My battery's low.	**b**	The reception here's terrible.
7	**a**	My connection went.	**b**	You're breaking up.
8	**a**	We got cut off	**b**	The reception here's terrible.
9	**a**	What are they saying?	**b**	You keep coming and going.

Get speaking

 1 Read the situations and think about what you might say in the conversations below. Then play the audio. Listen and respond when you hear the beeps.

13

1. You're at the airport. Ask if your friend heard the announcement.
2. You're talking on the Internet. Say what the communication problem is.
3. You're talking on the Internet again. Say what the communication problem is.
4. A friend calls your mobile. Apologize and say that your battery is low.
5. You're on your mobile. Explain that you're inside a building and the reception is poor.
6. You are talking to a friend on your mobile and the conversation ends suddenly. You call your friend back.

Everyday language

1 Look at Conversations 1–3 on pages 16–17 again. Find phrases with the meanings below.

Conversation 1	**Conversation 2**	**Conversation 3**
I can hear you well.	Here, where I am.	Is this call connected?

The answers to the exercise above are your Everyday language phrases for this unit. Go to page 88 to see these phrases in context. Then try to use them yourself.

Next steps

Try calling friends on the Internet or a mobile phone and practise speaking in English. It is likely you'll have at least some problems and get a chance to use some of the phrases in this unit!

4 EXCHANGING INFORMATION

Getting started

1 In what situations do you have to ask for information?
2 Do you ever have to do this in English?
3 What do you say if you can't follow all the information you're told?

Conversations

14

Read and listen to extracts from three conversations.

Conversation 1

Mark: So **I've had a chance to go through** the contract in detail and **I've got a couple of questions**.

Rhonda: Of course. What can I help you with?

Mark: Well, first, clause 25 … **Can you shed some light on** how that would affect us?

Rhonda: Well, basically, it just means you'll have to apply for an extended warranty once your standard warranty expires.

Mark: I see. **I take it** you'll be able to advise us further when the time comes?

Rhonda: Yes, our insurance department will be able to help you.

Mark: That does mean a lot of extra expense that we hadn't factored in. **I'll need some time to digest** all this. Can I get back to you later in the week?

Conversation 2

Receptionist: Good morning!

Ameera: Hi, I was just wondering, **I don't suppose you know** how much it costs to see a show on Broadway?

Receptionist: It really depends on the show. But here's a list of some of the options.

Ameera: Oh, wow! Expensive!

Receptionist: There's always off Broadway if you want something cheaper and a bit … different.

Ameera: **So you're saying** off Broadway plays are less pricy but a bit riskier for quality?

Receptionist: Mmm. It totally depends on the show.

Ameera:	Okay, thanks. **Have you got any idea** what the big shows are at the moment?
Receptionist:	Yeah, this list here is the top ten according to box office sales.
Ameera:	Oh, okay. Thanks, **that's very helpful.**
Receptionist:	No problem. If you need any help with buying tickets, just let me know.

Conversation 3

James:	You're through to James. How can I help?
Caller:	Oh, hi. My Internet banking password isn't being recognized and I've been locked out of my account.
James:	Okay, that's no problem. I can get a new password sent out to you.
Caller:	**Can you give me any idea** how long it'll take?
James:	It should be with you in five to ten working days.
Caller:	Oh. Er, is there anything you can do to speed it up?
James:	I'm afraid not, no. It's all the security, you see. You used to be able to go into your branch, and they'd do it on the spot, but it's all online now.
Caller:	Oh, okay. Let's do it now.
James:	Okay, I'll just take some details, and then I'll run you through what you have to do when your new password arrives …
	… and then once you've done that you'll be able to log in again.
Caller:	Sorry, **can you run that by me again?** First I need to log in with the password they send me ... **and then what?**
James:	Then there's an option to … . Then you can log in again.
Caller:	**Okay, I get it now, I think.**

Understanding

1 Look at the bold phrases in Conversations 1–3 and match them to strategies a–c.

a Asking for information b Checking information c Reacting to information

2 Answer the questions about Conversations 1–3.

1 Which speaker (Mark or Ameera) already has a lot of the information they need?

2 Which speaker (Mark or Ameera) sounds more confident?

3 Which of these questions sounds more confident?

   a I take it you know the manager? b I don't suppose you know the manager?

Saying it accurately

1 Complete the phrases with the words from the box.

run	get it	digest	some light	go through

1 Okay, I .... now, I think!

2 I've had a chance to .... the agreement in detail.

3 I'll need some time to .... all the facts and figures.

4 Can you shed .... on why the price is so high?

5 Sorry, can you .... that by me again?

2 Match phrases 1–6 from the conversations with phrases a–f that are used in a similar way.

1 I take it ...?   **a** Can you shed some light on ...?

2 I don't suppose you know ...?   **b** Can you give me any idea ...?

3 What happens next?   **c** And then what?

4 Can you run that by me again?   **d** So, basically ...

5 So you're saying ...?   **e** I presume ...?

6 Can you explain ...?   **f** Can you go over that again?

Saying it appropriately

1 Choose the most appropriate phrase for each situation.

1 You're talking to your flatmate.

   a Can you shed any light on the cinema times tonight?   **b** Have you got any idea what time the film's on tonight?

2 You've just been given the information you asked for at a museum.

   a That was very helpful.   **b** I'll need some time to digest the information.

3 Your friend has told you which train he's arriving on but you didn't catch what he said.

   a Run that by me again.   **b** I've got a couple of questions.

4 You're asking for information in your hotel.

   a I take it you know the best way to get to the airport?   **b** I don't suppose you know the best way to get to the airport?

 2 Listen to two versions of two sentences. Do speakers a or b sound impatient?

15

3 Listen to the impatient speakers again and underline the stressed word in each sentence.

1 Can you give me any idea where I can put my luggage?

2 And then what?

4 Listen to all the sentences again and repeat. Copy the sentence stress to sound polite or impatient.

Get speaking

16

1 Read the situations and think about what you might say in the conversations below. Then play the audio. Listen and respond when you hear the beeps.

1 You are about to sign a contract with a client at work.
- Say you've looked at the contract and have a few questions.
- Ask him about how long the delivery will take.
- Tell him you understand. Check that he will be able to confirm nearer the time.
- Ask for time to think about it all.

2 You want to visit a museum on the last afternoon of your holiday but don't know which one to choose. Ask at the hotel reception.
- Greet him and ask if he knows which nearby museum would be good for one afternoon.
- Say what kind of museum or gallery you'd be interested in and check if some of them are free.
- Ask if he knows if there are any special exhibitions on.
- End the conversation.

Everyday language

1 Look at Conversations 1–3 on pages 20–21 again. Find phrases with the meanings below.

| **Conversation 1** | Another good idea is … | **Conversation 3** |
| … when it happens. | I'll help you with … | at that exact time and location |

Conversation 2

The answers to the exercise above are your Everyday language phrases for this unit. Go to page 88 to see these phrases in context. Then try to use them yourself.

Next steps

Dealing with complicated information, or large amounts of new information, gets easier the more you do it. Why not practise by calling telephone information lines (e.g. for public transport, tourist attractions, ticket offices, etc.) in English-speaking countries? Use their websites to think about what you want to ask and then call and make your enquiry.

5 NEGOTIATING

Getting started

1 Negotiating isn't only a business skill. Can you think of examples of everyday negotiations?

2 What kinds of things do you need to negotiate about?

3 Are you a good negotiator?

Conversations

  Read and listen to extracts from three conversations.

17

Conversation 1

Seller: So, do you want to take this one?

Jim: Well, I'm definitely interested but **the price is higher than I was looking to pay.**

Seller: **What did you have in mind?**

Jim: Well, **what could you come down to?**

Seller: You know, it's a really gorgeous piece. You don't find many in such good condition either, so it's a pretty good price already.

Jim: I saw one on another stall that was a couple of hundred less, so maybe …

Seller: Well, **I might be willing to drop the price** by a hundred.

Jim: Knock off a hundred and fifty and I'll take it.

Seller: **Okay, go on then.** I think **you've got a deal.**

Conversation 2

Lana: Okay, so we're moving into the flat next week. How do you want to organize the bills?

Eva: Well, the TV and phone package is about the same as the water bill so **what if** you take one and I take the other? We'll be quits then.

Lana: Hmmm, okay, unless either of us makes calls abroad! Then there's the gas and electricity … but we've no idea how much they'll be. **How about if we** get a separate bank account just for bills?

Eva: Yeah, good idea! While we're on the subject, what about household stuff? You know, washing-up liquid and bits and bobs like that. I think **we should both chip in for** that stuff.

Lana: Yeah, we could have like a kitty for it and just put money in when it gets low.

Conversation 3

Builder: Hello?

Clive: Hi, I'm calling about some work I'm thinking of getting done. It's for some fencing – 20 metres and high enough to keep dogs out of our garden. Can you do me a quote for the job?

Builder: **You'd be looking at about** £250 depending on what finish we give the wood.

Clive: Ah, right. Er …**That seems like a lot**. It's only a small job. **Is that a fixed price?**

Builder: Well, like I said, it depends on the finish and I could always use a cheaper kind of wood.

Clive: So **what's the best price you can do** it for?

Builder: Let's see … £230.

Clive: I was thinking more like £180.

Builder: Huh! The materials alone would cost me that.

Clive: **Will you meet me in the middle?** Say, £210?

Builder: **Okay, done.**

Language note

In a negotiation about price, we don't usually say directly that something is too expensive. Instead, as in Conversations 1 and 3, we can say:

The price is **higher than I was looking to pay.**

That **seems like a lot.**

Understanding

① Look at the bold phrases in Conversations 1–3 and write them under the correct headings in the table below.

Opening a negotiation		Making an offer or a suggestion	
1	....	1	....
2	....	2	....
3	....	3	....
4	....	4	....
		5	....
Rejecting an offer		**Accepting an offer**	
1	....	1	....
2	....	2	....
		3	....

(2) When they are negotiating, speakers can sound sure and strong (firm) or unsure and hesitant (tentative). Look at the phrases you have written in the table in Exercise 1 and mark them T for *tentative* or F for *firm*.

(3) Look at Conversations 1–3 again and think about who has control of each conversation. Put an asterisk (*) by the sentences that you feel show control. When does control of the conversation change? Does it change back again? The answers can be quite subjective.

Saying it accurately

(1) Match the sentence halves.

1	What did you have …		**a**	in the middle?
2	What could you come …		**b**	best price you can do?
3	I might be willing to …		**c**	looking to pay.
4	Is that a fixed …		**d**	price?
5	Will you meet me …		**e**	in mind?
6	We should both chip …		**f**	in for cleaning supplies.
7	The price is higher than I was …		**g**	a deal.
8	What's the …		**h**	down to?
9	You've got …		**i**	drop the price by a few dollars.

(2) Complete the sentences with the words from the box. You can use some words more than once. There is one extra word that you don't need.

1 That's higher than I was looking .... pay.

2 What did you have .... mind?

3 What could you come .... to?

4 I might be willing to drop the price .... £20.

5 We should both chip .... for Dave's leaving present.

6 How .... if we split all the bills equally?

off
to
by
in
about
down

Saying it appropriately

18

(1) When you're negotiating, you can turn a question back onto the other person just by stressing the words differently. Read and listen to two conversations and underline the stressed word in the second question.

1 At a secondhand car dealer's

Customer: I might be interested in buying this one. What price did you have in mind?

Seller: What price did you have in mind?

Customer: Well, that depends …

2 Two flatmates are discussing housework.

Bob: I'll clean the kitchen so how about if you do the bathroom?

Tina: How about if you do the bathroom? I did it last week!

2 Listen again and repeat the second questions. Copy the stress to turn the question back onto the other person.

19

3 Some negotiation phrases are tentative, while others are firmer. But intonation also affects how tentative or firm you sound. Listen to these sentences and decide which speakers sound the most tentative.

1 You'd be looking at about two to three months.
2 You'd be looking at about two to three months.
3 The price is higher than I was looking to pay.
4 The price is higher than I was looking to pay.

4 Listen to the sentences again and repeat. Copy the stress and intonation to sound either firm or tentative.

Get speaking

20

1 Read the situations and think about what you might say in the conversations below. Then play the audio. Listen and respond when you hear the beeps.

1 You're interested in buying a second-hand car. Try to negotiate with the salesman.

- Tell him that you're interested but the price is too high for you.
- Try to get him to name a price.
- Ask if a price reduction is possible.
- Try to get a lower price and say you'll take it.

2 You're discussing arrangements with your future flatmate.

- Suggest splitting the bills.   • Make a suggestion.   • Accept her suggestion.

Everyday language

1 Look at Conversations 2–3 on pages 24 25 again. Find phrases with the meanings below.

Conversation 2

We won't owe each other anything any more.

I'm trying to sound like I'm mentioning this casually …

small things

Conversation 3

I'm reminding you I said this before …

I had a different idea in mind.

The answers to the exercise above are your Everyday language phrases for this unit. Go to page 89 to see these phrases in context. Then try to use them yourself.

Next steps

TV shows in which people buy and sell things are good places to hear language to do with negotiating. Try searching online to find clips from series such as *The Apprentice* to hear this language in action.

6 INTERRUPTING AND LETTING OTHERS SPEAK

Getting started

1 Is it acceptable to interrupt other people in your culture?
2 In what situations do you find it difficult to interrupt and make yourself heard in English?

Conversations

21

1   Read and listen to extracts from three conversations.

Conversation 1

Fran: We really need to get everything sorted for this fundraiser. Time's ticking away.

Danny: Mmmm, only two weeks to go.

Mal: Yeah, I guess it's …

Fran: Exactly. Now, the venue's booked but we've got to find a caterer and print up flyers.

Danny: And the newspaper ad.

Mal: Well, I was thinking …

Fran: Flyers are going to be expensive …

Mal: Yes, that's why I was going to …

Fran: … even the places on the uni campus aren't cheap.

Mal: **Sorry, can I say something?**

Fran: **Sorry, what were you saying?**

Danny: **Go on.**

Mal: How about just using social media to advertise? The university has loads of forums we can promote ourselves on.

Conversation 2

Pierre: Josh, I'm home. And Regan's here!

Josh: Hey, Regan!

Pierre: Hey, this place is a tip!

Josh: Um, I think you'll find it's your gym stuff all over the floor not mine!

Regan: So guys, what's for dinner?

Pierre:	So, whose trainers are these then, huh?
Josh:	Okay, and this towel? And those shorts? And that …
Regan:	**If I can get a word in edgewise …**
Pierre:	Oh! Really sorry, Regan. How rude of us! **Go ahead.**
Josh:	**Sorry, got carried away there.**
Regan:	**I was just wondering**, seeing as you've invited me round for dinner, what you're planning to cook me since all I can see in the fridge are three bananas and a load of tomatoes.
Pierre:	I thought you were getting groceries!
Josh:	I did! I just haven't unpacked the car yet!

Conversation 3

Jamie:	Right, so we're agreed on Item 1 then, Leah? Heidi?
Heidi:	Yeah, I think …
Jamie:	The budget committee head will be Sara from June 1. Which brings us to Item 2: Health and Safety. Leah?
Leah:	Thank you. Yes, it seems parents are concerned about the crossing outside the school. The road's really busy now so maybe we should hire someone to help children across.
Jamie:	Well, we can't argue with that. Safety has to be our priority.
Leah:	Of course!
Heidi:	Well, I …
Jamie:	Parents have to feel their children are safe both in school and on the way to and from here.
Leah:	I agree.
Heidi:	Sorry, **can I just ask a question?** Do we have the money for this in this year's budget?
Jamie:	I think we can find it from somewhere for something as important as this!
Heidi:	Yes, but …
Leah:	Surely we can …
Heidi:	**After you, sorry.**
Leah:	**No, no, after you.**
Heidi:	**I just wanted to say** if we employ someone from September, it can go on next year's budget and we could maybe cover it with teachers in the meantime.
Leah:	Oh, good idea!
Jamie:	Yes, Heidi, great. Item 2 settled then. On to Item 3.

Understanding

1 Answer the questions about Conversations 1–3.

  1 Which people were trying to be heard in each conversation?

  2 Did the other people let them speak?

2 Look at the bold phrases in Conversations 1–3 and match them to the correct strategies a–c below.

  a Making yourself heard   **b** Making your point   **c** Letting someone speak

3 Match phrases 1–4 to phrases a–d which have a similar meaning.

  1 Go ahead.   **a** If I can get a word in edgeways.

  2 After you, sorry.   **b** I was just wondering …

  3 Can I just ask something?   **c** Go on.

  4 Can someone let me speak?   **d** Sorry, what were you saying?

Saying it accurately

1 Complete the phrases with the words from the box. There are two words that you don't need.

after	on	away	around	over	after	ahead

  1 Go ....   **4** Go ....

  2 Sorry, got carried .... there.   **5** No, no .... you.

  3 .... you, sorry.

Saying it appropriately

1 Listen to the intonation of two speakers interrupting politely. Is the intonation rising or falling?

  1 Can I just ask a question?   **2** Can I say something?

2 Listen again and repeat. Copy the intonation to sound polite.

3 Choose the most polite way to interrupt in the following situations. Sometimes both options are correct.

  1 You're making holiday plans with friends.

    Claire: Well, I think Morocco or Turkey. They're both cheap once you get there. We just have to pay for the flights and then everything else is cheap. And the accommodation is really easy to find. And the food is amazing. I've …

    You:

    a If I can get a word in edgeways, I was thinking further away … like Asia.

    b Can I just say something? I was thinking further away … like Asia.

    c Both

2 You're in a meeting at work. Someone is dominating a discussion and not letting anyone else speak.

> **Richard:** So, I think we will all agree that the best time to have our next meeting is Sunday at 15:00. I've reserved a meeting room already. I brainstormed ideas for the theme of the campaign and I liked '70s Disco' best so we'll go with that. James, you're good with …

You:

a Can you let me speak! Are we all agreed on the 70s theme?

b Can I just ask something? Are we all agreed on the 70s theme?

c Both

Get speaking

1 Play the audio and listen to the people in the situations below. Choose a polite place to interrupt and pause the audio. Use an appropriate phrase.

1 Your friend is talking about something that happened to her at work. You want to ask what other people in the meeting thought.

2 A tour guide is showing you round a palace. You want to say that you thought the palace was older than that.

2 You are going to talk about the three topics below but someone will interrupt you. Press play and start talking. When the person interrupts, use phrases from the unit to let them speak.

1 Start talking about your hometown.

2 Start talking about your last holiday.

3 Start telling a friend about what you're going to do this weekend.

Everyday language

1 Look at Conversations 1–3 again. Find phrases with the meanings below.

Conversation 1

only … weeks until then.

Conversation 2

We're very … !

Conversation 3

Now it's time to discuss …

It's difficult to disagree with …

on the journey to a place and back again

while we're waiting for something to happen

The answers to the exercise above are your Everyday language phrases for this unit. Go to page 89 to see these phrases in context. Then try to use them yourself.

Next steps

To see how people interact in groups and make their voices heard, try watching political debate programmes like *Question Time* or *Real Time* on YouTube.

---

7 SHOWING INTEREST

Getting started

1 Can you remember a conversation where someone seemed uninterested in what you were saying?
2 What made you think this?
3 How can you show interest with body language and words?

Conversations

25

1 Read and listen to extracts from four conversations.

Conversation 1

Georgia: ... and the thing is I'd been at work all day and then we had a 15-hour flight to deal with. It was really tiring.

Debbie: Oh, **exhausting!**

Georgia: The plane was one of those new ones with two floors, so the kids were excited and running around all the time and I was getting stressed because I was so tired ...

Debbie: **Yeah.**

Georgia: ... and I ended up shouting at them and bursting into tears at customs. But it had been such a long day.

Debbie: **Of course, 15 hours** on a plane is enough to make anyone lose their temper, let alone someone travelling with two small kids.

Georgia: Mmm, and poor Mike! I was awful company ...

Debbie: Well, that's what husbands are for, isn't it?

Conversation 2

Jack: ... The monkeys were the best for photos because they came up so close. They ate out of our hands.

Helen: Aaaw! **How cute!**

Jack: One even stole my sunglasses – snatched them right out of my hands.

Helen: **No way! Wasn't there some kind of keeper or someone?**

Jack: Yeah, but he said it was because they were yellow, so they looked like a banana.

Helen: **Ah, right! Did you get them back?**

Jack: Nah, monkeys bite if you corner them. I just took a photo. Look!

Helen: Aaaw, yeah, so many pictures ...

Jack: **Hundreds, yeah ...**

Conversation 3

Greg: The more houses I look at, the less I know what I want. I'm not even sure if I want to live in the suburbs or the city centre.

Michelle: Mmm. **Suburbs or city centre.** Yeah, that's a tough one. There's so many advantages to both. Have you tried making a list of pros and cons?

Greg: Mmm. **A list** … yeah that's not a bad idea.

Michelle: If it's any help, I'm much happier since I got out of the centre.

Greg: **Are you?** Really? **Why's that?**

Michelle: Well, I finish work and I get the bus home and I see the park and the green, you know? And I can just really disconnect from work. And if I want to buy something I can go to the local shop, instead of some anonymous supermarket chain.

Greg: Yeah. **Disconnecting from work.** I could definitely use some of that.

Conversation 4

Marjorie: Thank you for coming, dear. It's very thoughtful of you.

Alex: **Thoughtful?** No, it's nothing, come on! Er, I've bought you some tulips.

Marjorie: Oh, **flowers!** How lovely! They're a beautiful colour.

Alex: Yeah. **Red and purple,** your favourite. I remembered.

Marjorie: Yes! Let's see if one of the nurses can put them in a vase for me …

Speaking tip: strategies for showing interest

In this unit, the phrases in bold are not key phrases, but examples of strategies for showing interest. There are different strategies for showing interest:

- asking questions to get more information
- using short questions
- echoing by repeating part of the other speaker's sentence
- using a synonym or word with a similar meaning

We use echoing strategies to establish common ground and make the other speaker feel good. We only use echoing in informal situations, when we want to make an effort to show someone that we're listening and interested in them.

Understanding

1 Look at the bold phrases in Conversations 1–4. Find three examples of each strategy a–c below.

a Asking questions   **b** Echoing by repeating   **c** Using synonyms

2 There is one more strategy for showing interest. All the conversations show people using exclamations. Underline all the exclamations you can find in Conversations 1–4.

3 Match one of the exclamations you found for Exercise 2 to each category 1–5 below. Then number the exclamations in the box according to their category.

1	Expressing surprise	**3**	Expressing sympathy	**5**	Expressing understanding
2	Expressing approval	**4**	Expressing agreement		

You're kidding!	Fantastic!	Ah, I get it now.
Absolutely.	Wow!	That's brilliant news!
Oh, shame.	That's unbelievable!	I don't believe it!

Saying it accurately

1 Choose the correct short questions from the box to follow the sentences below.

Did you?	Has he?	Have you?	Is he?	Did I?	Am I?

1 **A:** I've really missed Spanish food since I moved to England.   **B:** ....
2 **A:** Aren't you the one who wanted to try spicy food?   **B:** ....
3 **A:** He's been talking about writing a book for ages.   **B:** ....

2 Choose a word or phrase to echo in these sentences. There is more than one right answer.

1 We've got it all planned. The wedding's going to be in my village and the reception's in my old school. It's perfect!

2 I'm applying to two of the top law universities but I don't think I'll get in. You need really high grades and I'm doing okay, but not well enough. We'll see!

3 We ate out every day when we lived there. There was a great Italian around the corner. And a Chinese with a really cheap lunch deal. London can be really good value when you know where to go.

Saying it appropriately

1 Intonation is very important when showing interest. Listen to two versions (a and b) of four conversations 1–4 and say whether the speakers sound interested or uninterested.

2 Tone of voice is also important. Listen to two versions (a and b) of two conversations and say which speakers sound sincere when they respond.

3 Listen again to the interested and sincere phrases. Repeat the phrases, copying the intonation and tone of voice to sound interested and sincere.

1	Really?	**3**	Aren't you?	**5**	Good idea!
2	Fiji, very nice!	**4**	You're really busy.		

4 Choose an appropriate exclamation from the box to follow these sentences. Sometimes more than one answer is possible.

You're kidding!	Oh, shame.	Wow!
Absolutely.	Fantastic!	I don't believe it!

1 A: I just found out I passed all my exams!   **B:** ....
2 A: Sue's parents got her a car for her 21st birthday.   **B:** ....
3 A: It's not right to leave a dog alone in the house all day.   **B:** ....
4 A: I can't come tonight – I've got to finish some work.   **B:** ....

Get speaking

 Play the audio. Listen to five one-sided conversations and respond to show interest when you hear the beeps. Lots of strategies are possible, so, if the first time you use exclamations, try again with echoing or asking questions.

1 Heidi is telling you about her holiday.

2 Craig is telling you about a bad experience he had in a restaurant.

3 Nadya is telling you about a decision she has to make about a new job.

4 You're talking to your friend Felix about films.

5 You're talking to Stephen about his weekend plans.

Everyday language

1 Find phrases 1–4 below in Conversations 1–3 on pages 32–33. Use the context to help you choose meaning a or b.

Conversation 1

1 is enough to make anyone …
   a Most people wouldn't react in this way.   **b** Anyone would react in the same way.

2 let alone …
   a … is even more difficult.   **b** … is easier.

3 That's what … are for!
   a That's one bad thing about having …   **b** That's one good thing about having …

Conversation 3

4 If it's any help, …
   a I'm going to ask you something.   **b** I'm going to tell you something useful.

The answers to the exercise above are your Everyday language phrases for this unit. Go to page 89 to see these phrases in context. Then try to use them yourself.

Next steps

Watch TV interviews where two people are talking and notice how they show interest and keep the conversation moving. You can often download transcripts so you can analyse conversations too.

8 BEING SUPPORTIVE

Getting started

1 How do you cheer yourself up if you're having a bad day?
2 What do you say to make someone else feel better if they're having a bad day?

Conversations

1 Read and listen to extracts from four conversations.

Conversation 1

Pietr: Hi! What are you …? Uh oh, **is something wrong?**

Sean: Remember that course I was waiting to hear about? I didn't get a place.

Pietr: Oh no!

Sean: I'm on some waiting list which I bet is as long as my arm.

Pietr: Oh well then … . **Maybe it's not as bad as you think.** It doesn't start till September, right? Loads of people will probably have dropped out by then.

Sean: Do you think so?

Pietr: Yeah, definitely! I got into my university like that. But apply to some other places anyway. **Something's bound to work out sooner or later.**

Conversation 2

Mohammed: **Are you okay? You don't seem your usual self**, Scott.

Scott: I know it sounds stupid but I'm really missing my family at the moment.

Mohammed: That's not stupid. **Everyone feels like that sometimes.** Even me – my family are only a couple of hours away.

Scott: Mmmm, yeah. I think it's just crept up on me because it's my mum's birthday tomorrow and I know the whole family will be there.

Mohammed: Ah, well. Just keep busy and **do something to take your mind off it**. Why don't you come out with me and the lads tonight?

Scott: Yeah, thanks, that sounds good. And you're right. I can always video call them tomorrow – see them all.

Mohammed: Exactly. **You'll feel much better then!**

Conversation 3

Kathryn: Hey, how's it going?

Malcolm: Ugh, shouldn't complain, I know, but I'm flat out with work at the minute. I've barely had a minute to myself for weeks and it's starting to stress me out.

Kathryn: Really? **Sorry to hear that**. It can't last forever, though. And **look on the bright side**. At least you must be feeling rich if you've got so much work on. Every cloud …

Conversation 4

Rana: I'm really worried about all these letters I've been getting from the tax people.

Colin: Yeah, I hate tax. **It's a nightmare.**

Rana: Yeah. They say I owe them a fortune but I know that can't be right. Whenever I call them I can't get through to anyone, and then I get another letter.

Colin: **Maybe** speaking to an accountant **would set your mind at rest.**

Rana: Yeah, I've got an appointment to see a woman tomorrow actually.

Colin: Oh, good. Then **try and put it out of your mind**. Don't worry. **I'm sure it'll all get sorted out in the end.**

Understanding

① Look at the bold phrases in Conversations 1–4 and write them in the correct sections of the table below.

Finding out if someone's okay	Expressing sympathy
1	1 ....
2	2 ....
3	3 ....
Being positive	**Giving advice**
1	1 ....
2	2 ....
3	3 ....
4	
5	

Saying it accurately

1 Match the sentence halves.

1	Do something to …	**a**	bright side.
2	Maybe it's not as …	**b**	your usual self.
3	Look on the …	**c**	out of your mind.
4	Try and put it …	**d**	your mind at rest.
5	Maybe … would set …	**e**	take your mind off it.
6	Something's bound to …	**f**	work out sooner or later.
7	You don't seem …	**g**	bad as you think.

2 Complete the sentences with the words from the box. You can use the words more than once. There are two words you won't need.

out	on	to	at	in	up	off

1 Do something to take your mind .... it.

2 Look .... the bright side.

3 Try and put it .... of your mind.

4 Maybe … would set your mind .... rest.

5 I'm sure it'll all get sorted out .... the end.

6 Something's bound to work .... sooner or later.

Saying it appropriately

31

1 Intonation is important when you are being supportive. Read and listen to the sentences and underline the words that are stressed.

1 You don't seem your usual self.

2 Sorry to hear that.

3 I'm sure it'll all get sorted out in the end.

4 Something's bound to work out sooner or later.

5 Maybe it's not as bad as you think.

6 Do something to take your mind off it.

7 Look on the bright side.

8 Try and put it out of your mind.

9 Maybe speaking to a doctor would set your mind at rest.

2 Listen to the sentences in Exercise 1 again and repeat. Copy the intonation to sound supportive.

3 Read the situations below. Choose the response which is the most suitable and supportive.

1 Your colleague tells you a relative has just died.

    a I'm sorry to hear that.   **b** Try and do something to take your mind off it.

2 Your flatmate has just failed an exam at university and might have to retake the year.

    a Look on the bright side.   **b** Maybe speaking to your tutor would set your mind at rest.

3 A friend is having problems finding someone to repair their car.

    a Try and put it out of your mind.   **b** I'm sure it'll all get sorted out in the end.

Speaking tip: asking questions

Asking questions is another way of being supportive. However, there's a fine line between asking enough questions to be supportive and being insensitive by asking too many. Keep your questions general, or express sympathy with phrases like 'Sorry to hear that'. The person will say more if they want to.

Get speaking

32

1 Read the situations and think about what you might say in the conversations below. Then play the audio. Listen and respond when you hear the beeps.

1 You arrive at work and see a colleague looking worried.

- Say something to start a conversation to find out if anything's wrong.
- Express sympathy.
- Be positive and give advice.

2 A friend has recently received some bad news about a family member. You don't know the details but want to offer support.

- Start the conversation by asking if there's a problem.
- Express sympathy and be positive.
- Give some advice.

Everyday language

1 Look at Conversations 1–3 on pages 36–37 again. Find phrases with the meanings below.

Conversation 1	**Conversation 2**	**Conversation 3**
very long	I want to say something but I'm worried you'll think badly of me.	I'm really busy with …
	I've just realized very slowly.	I haven't had time to do anything at all for weeks.

The answers to the exercise above are your Everyday language phrases for this unit. Go to page 89 to see these phrases in context. Then try to use them yourself.

Next steps

Chat show hosts tend to be supportive towards guests if they're revealing problems. Record these kinds of TV shows and then practise some of the language in this unit as if you're the host.

9 PERSUASION

Getting started

1 Are you good at persuading people to do things?
2 Do you have strong willpower or do you give in easily?
3 Are there situations when you have to give in so that you don't offend people?

Conversations

  Read and listen to extracts from four conversations.

> **Conversation 1**
>
> **Simon:** How do you feel about doing something different this summer? We could go on a cycling holiday round France – do something active for a change.
>
> **Penny:** If you want to go cycling, we'd be as well to stay in Scotland. It's great for that here.
>
> **Simon:** Yeah, but the weather's bound to be a problem. So, you'd consider a cycling holiday then?
>
> **Penny:** I didn't say that exactly. **It's not really my thing.**
>
> **Simon:** **How do you know if you've never tried?**
>
> **Penny:** I just know, okay, so **there's no point trying to talk me into it**. I just want to relax on a beach somewhere, not cycle 10,000 miles a day!
>
> **Simon:** But **you have to admit** you were bored last summer.
>
> **Penny:** Did I say that?
>
> **Simon:** Only every day! **Will you at least think about it?**
>
> **Penny:** I'm really not interested in cycling, sorry.
>
> **Simon:** Okay, **have it your own way.** The beach, as always.

> **Conversation 2**
>
> **Jean:** I've got an extra ticket to the theatre tonight. Fancy coming?
>
> **Maggie:** Oh ... I've got way too much work to do. I really can't, sorry.
>
> **Jean:** **Oh, go on!** All work and no play ...
>
> **Maggie:** **Yeah**, I know but I'm way behind on everything.
>
> **Jean:** Yeah, but **you might not get the chance again.** Final show tonight ...

Maggie: Well, **I suppose it can't hurt** to take one night off.

Jean: Great! I didn't think you'd cave in anywhere near as easily as that!

Maggie: What can I say? I'm such a pushover!

Language note

'All work and no play …' is the first half of a longer saying, 'All work and no play makes Jack a dull boy'. Some sayings are so well known that you don't need to finish them, because everyone will understand them. Other examples are 'When in Rome …' ('… do as the Romans do.') and 'Every cloud …' ('… has a silver lining.') from Unit 8.

Conversation 3

Anya: I see you eyeing up my ice cream. Just have some if you want.

Brenda: I can't. I've been so good this week.

Anya: Well, **one** bite **won't hurt then, will it?**

Brenda: **I really shouldn't …**

Anya: Go on, **you know you want to.**

Brenda: Oh, okay! **You've twisted my arm.** But just a spoonful!

Conversation 4

Oliver: Yeah, I know, but it **makes more sense** to skip your Mum's and get back home in time for the football.

Mimi: **Wouldn't it be easier to** just watch the game at Mum's?

Oliver: Yeah, but her TV is too small to watch it properly. And it means you'd be driving home really late.

Mimi: That's true.

Oliver: That's settled then!

Mimi: **It doesn't sound like I've got much choice!**

Understanding

1 Sometimes people refuse to do things because they think they shouldn't do them. At other times they refuse because they don't *want* to do them. Look at Conversations 1–4 and answer the questions.

1   Which two speakers give in happily? ....

2   Are they being persuaded to do something they think they shouldn't, or something they don't want to do? ....

2 Look at Conversations 1–4 again and find phrases for strategies a–d below.

a Persuading someone to do something   **c** Being persuaded reluctantly

b Being persuaded happily   **d** Refusing to be persuaded

Cultural note

In many countries being too forceful when trying to persuade someone is aggressive. Using questions makes the persuasion feel less strong, e.g. 'Wouldn't it be easier to …?' 'How do you know if you've never…?' 'One bite won't hurt, will it?'.

Saying it accurately

1 Match the phrases below to categories a–d in Understanding Exercise 2.

1 Can I twist your arm to …? ……

2 Can I tempt you to …? ……

3 Go on then! ……

4 Can I talk you into …? ……

5 How can I say no? ……

6 It's not for me. ……

2 Complete the phrases with the words from the box.

Persuading people

1 Can I ………………… your arm to help me?

2 Can I ………………… you to …?

3 You know you ………………… to!

4 You'd be better ………………… walking than driving there.

5 How do you ………………… if you've never tried?

Being persuaded or refusing

6 Go ………………… then!

7 Okay, have it your own ………………… .

8 It's not really my ………………… .

9 There's no ………………… trying to talk me into it.

10 It's not ………………… me.

| off |
| twist |
| on |
| thing |
| for |
| tempt |
| point |
| know |
| way |
| want |

Saying it appropriately

34

1 Listen to the stress in the questions below. Underline the stressed words. Which speaker sounds annoyed, and which sounds persuasive?

1 Will you at least think about it?   **2** Will you at least think about it?

2 Listen again and repeat, copying the stress to sound annoyed or persuasive.

35

3 Listen to the intonation in another pair of phrases. Which speaker sounds persuasive? Which speaker has been persuaded and is giving in?

1 Oh, go on!   **2** Oh, go on!

4   Listen again and repeat the phrases, copying the intonation firstly to sound persuasive and then to show that you have been persuaded and are giving in.

Get speaking

36

1   Read the situations and think about what you might say in the conversations below. Then play the audio. Listen and respond when you hear the beeps.

1   You're talking to your roommate. She's got a lot of work to do but you want to go out.
- Invite your roommate to the cinema tonight.
- Try to persuade her.
- She's on the point of saying yes, so give her the last bit of persuasion she needs.
- Show you are pleased she has changed her mind.

2   You're trying to persuade your friend to go on a skiing trip but he prefers holidays in hot countries.
- Introduce the idea of skiing and suggest a skiing holiday.
- Try to persuade him to give it a try.
- Try to persuade him again using a different argument.

3   You're in a café with a friend. You've had a lot of coffee today, and you know you shouldn't drink too much, but you love it.
- Refuse the coffee.
- Try not to give in to temptation.
- Be persuaded and give in!

4   Have the conversation for situation 3 again, but this time don't give in.

Everyday language

1   Look at Conversations 1–4 on pages 40–41 again. Find phrases with the meanings below.

Conversation 1

Every time is the same.

Conversation 2

It's easy to convince me!

Conversation 3

I know you want my …

Conversation 4

That's the end of this argument or discussion.

The answers to the exercise above are your Everyday language phrases for this unit. Go to pages 89–90 to see these phrases in context. Then try to use them yourself.

Next steps

Read the Language note on page 41 again. Then think of sayings you know in English and see if there is a logical way to cut them in half. Try to use them in conversation.

10 BEING TACTFUL

Getting started

1   How tactful are you?
2   Can you think of someone who is quite direct with their opinions?
3   What situations call for more tact?

Conversations

37

Read and listen to extracts from four conversations.

Conversation 1

Ayla:	How about this one?
Nadine:	It's very ... er ... bright!
Ayla:	Yeah! I need something for Mike's wedding in June. What do you think?
Nadine:	Well ... **I'm not sure it's your colour.** Or **it's not quite the right style for you** or something.
Ayla:	You mean you don't like it!
Nadine:	**It's not that. I just think** you looked great in that pink one you tried before.
Ayla:	Do you think so?

Conversation 2

Martin:	Here we go. Two hours slaving in the kitchen and voila! Roast chicken! It's a bit burnt around the edges but it'll be fine inside!
Jason and Linda:	Ohhh!
Linda:	**It's not *that* burnt.**
Jason:	Lovely ...
Martin:	Help yourselves!
Jason:	Not too much for me, thanks, I'm trying to watch the old waistline.
Linda:	**It smells lovely but** I'm not that hungry either.
Martin:	More for me then! ... So?
Jason:	**It's ... got an interesting flavour** ... what herbs did you use?

| Martin: | Oh, a bit of everything. Whatever I had in the cupboard. Linda, what do you think? |
| Linda: | **Not bad for a first attempt,** Martin! **Maybe it's a tad salty though.** Could I have some more water? |

Conversation 3

Clara:	So, now you've finally met Harry, what do you think? Isn't he great?
Ahmed:	Ah ...
Clara:	What?
Ahmed:	**It's really none of my business,** and if you're happy ...
Clara:	If you've got something to say, just say it!
Ahmed:	**He's just not exactly who** I imagined you'd end up with, that's all.
Clara:	How do you mean?
Ahmed:	He's a bit ... er, direct.
Clara:	Are you trying to say he's rude?
Ahmed:	**I wouldn't say** rude **exactly, but** he is quite, er ... forceful, **let's say.**
Clara:	Ha! Don't worry. You're not the first person to say that. It drives me mad too.
Ahmed:	Good! Is the interrogation over now?

Conversation 4

Gillian:	Thanks for getting the proposal in on time.
Adam:	No problem. Does it look okay?
Gillian:	Ah ... yeah. **There are plenty of positive things** in it.
Adam:	Uh oh. I can feel a 'but' coming.
Gillian:	**It's nothing major** but there are some parts that **need a bit more work.**
Adam:	Hmm, okay. Such as?
Gillian:	Actually, it's mainly just the conclusion that's **not quite right.** And I put some notes in some places to show you where you could tidy it up a bit. We can go over it later if you like.

Cultural note

In some cultures it's acceptable to be direct with your opinions. In others, even when someone asks for your opinion, it's better to be tactful and avoid answering directly.

In British and American culture for example, it is usually acceptable to say 'You look tired' but it would be seen as tactless to comment if a friend had gained weight or was dressed in a way you didn't like.

Understanding

1 Look at the bold phrases in Conversations 1–4 and write them in the correct sections of the table below.

Downplaying negative qualities	Emphasizing positive qualities
1	1 ....
2	2 ....
3	3 ....
4	4 ....
5	
6	
Giving your opinion in an indirect way	**Avoiding giving an opinion**
1	1 ....
2	
3	
4	

Saying it accurately

1 Complete the tactful phrases with words from the box.

1 Not bad for a .... !
2 I wouldn't say freezing exactly but quite cold, ...
3 It's really none of ....
4 It's not .... style for you.
5 It needs .... more work.
6 Maybe it's .... undercooked.
7 It's just .... what I was expecting.
8 There are .... positive things in it.

> not exactly
> first attempt
> plenty of
> let's say
> a bit
> a tad
> quite the right
> my business

Saying it appropriately

1 Which tactful phrases could replace the very direct ones below?

1 That dress doesn't suit you.
2 It's too salty.
3 I don't like this soup.
4 I don't like him.
5 He's rude.
6 This report isn't good enough.

2 What would you say in these situations to be tactful?

1 A friend asks you about the décor in their flat and you think it's far too bright.
It's not exactly ....
2 Someone asks what you think of your new team captain. You think he's underqualified.
He's just not exactly who ....

3 A friend asks what you think of the dress she wants to buy. You think it's too tight for her.

I'm not sure ....

4 Someone asks you what you think of a mutual friend's new husband. You don't like him at all.

It's really ....

5 A colleague has asked you to look at their presentation. You think it doesn't make sense but don't want to criticize it too much.

There are a lot .... Maybe it ....

Get speaking

1 Read the situations and think about what you might say in the conversations below. Then play the audio. Listen and respond when you hear the beeps.

1 A friend is showing you a bag that she has made. You don't really like it.

- Be tactful, and try to think of something nice to say about the bag.
- Be tactful.
- Find a tactful way to say no thanks.

2 Your friend has just cooked you a meal, but it isn't very nice.

- Be grateful and show tactful appreciation.
- Give a tactful reply.

3 Someone asks you about a new colleague at work. You think she's arrogant and lazy. Be tactful.

- Say something tactful and general.
- When pressed for detail, be tactful but a bit more specific.

4 A work colleague asked you to read a report they wrote. It isn't very good and half of it needs rewriting.

- Emphasize the positive.
- Tactfully tell him there are some problems.

Everyday language

1 Look at Conversations 2–4 on pages 44–45 again. Find phrases with the meanings below.

Conversation 2	Conversation 3	Conversation 4
working hard cooking	Other people have said that.	I think you're going to say
I'm on a diet.		something I won't like.
		Can you give me an example?

The answers to the exercise above are your Everyday language phrases for this unit. Go to page 90 to see these phrases in context. Then try to use them yourself.

Next steps

Next time you give a piece of work to your teacher to correct, ask them directly what they thought of it and listen carefully to the feedback they give you. Are they being tactful?

If you have English-speaking friends, ask their opinions about your clothes!

11 ADMITTING AND DENYING

Getting started

1 What kinds of mistake should you admit immediately?
2 If it's not your fault, would you blame someone else?
3 Do you usually make excuses or just apologize?

Conversations

39

Read and listen to extracts from four conversations.

Conversation 1

Elise: Oh no! Look at the state of this place! I told you to make sure this door was locked.

Derek: **Don't look at me**. Listen, **I wasn't the last one** to come in here!

Elise: Yes, you were. You came in to get that book.

Derek: Oh … I was sure I closed the door, though.

Elise: How many times do I have to tell you? You have to lock it as well. Jerry can open it himself otherwise.

Derek: Well, **it's not all my fault**. I mean, **I'm not the one who** has all this paint lying around everywhere.

Elise: So you're blaming me because I'm the artist, when, if you'd locked the door, we wouldn't have this mess?

Derek: … how difficult is it to put a lid on?

Elise: What did you say?

Derek: I said, 'Let's clear this mess up'.

Conversation 2

Ardal: … she was really angry. I wouldn't like to be in your shoes when she finds out it was you.

Chong: Do you think **I should just own up** now? Get it over with?

Ardal: Well, maybe.

Chong: I really didn't know she still wanted those paintings. **I'd never have** thrown them away **if I'd known**.

Ardal: I'd just **come clean**, say it was you and tell her you're sorry and you'll try to get them back or buy her some new ones or something.

Chong: Yeah, you're right. Wish me luck!

Conversation 3

Dean: Hey, I got the phone bill today and it's three times what we normally pay. So I checked and there are all these long distance calls to Australia.

Leila: Uh oh. **I hold my hands up**. Those were mine.

Dean: Why didn't you buy one of those international calling cards or use Skype or something?

Leila: **In my defence**, I thought we had a deal on the phone and we got free calls to certain countries. I'm sure I remember you saying that.

Dean: Yeah, we do have a deal, but we have free calls to America, not Australia.

Leila: I mean, **I'm not trying to get out of it, but** I'm sure I said something about how perfectly that worked for me and you agreed.

Dean: Why would I have said Australia when I know it's America? I haven't got a clue about calling Australia!

Leila: Whatever. There's no point arguing about it. How much is it?

Conversation 4

Annabel: What's going on here? Why are you in my room? Keira!

Keira: **It's not how it looks!**

Annabel: It better not be! You're in my room without permission, wearing my clothes … and … making a complete mess!

Keira: Yeah, I know, but **I can explain!** You see, **the thing is**, it's supposed to be a surprise for your birthday …

Annabel: You're taking my clothes without asking, as a present? You must think I'm an idiot!

Keira: No! **I was just** trying them on because there's this outfit I wanted to buy you and I thought I could check the size on myself first and then …

Annabel: Seriously, Keira. Don't you think it might've been easier to just look at the labels?

Keira: Oh … yeah …

Understanding

1 Look at Conversations 1–4 again. Find two people who do the things a–c below.

a Admit responsibility: ....

b Make excuses: ....

c Deny responsibility and try to blame someone else: ....

2 Look at the bold phrases in Conversations 1–4 and match them to the correct strategies a–c below.

    a Admitting   **b** Making excuses   **c** Denying and blaming someone else

Saying it accurately

1 Complete the sentences with the words from the box.

out of	look	hold	clean	fault	thing	defence	own

1 It's not all my .... we're lost! It was you who forgot the maps!
2 I know the report's late but, in my ...., I have been ill.
3 I should come .... It was me that left the oven on. Sorry.
4 I suppose you're right. If I just .... up, it'll be easier in the long run.
5 I'm not trying to get .... it but wasn't it you that forgot to pay the insurance?
6 You see, the .... is, it wasn't me that wrote that, it was Simon.
7 I .... my hands up. I made a mistake with the dates.
8 Don't .... at me! It was like that when I found it!

Saying it appropriately

40

1 Listen to two people denying something and blaming someone else. Underline the stressed words.

1 It's not my fault we're lost!
2 I wasn't the last one to use the oven!

2 Listen again and repeat. Copy the stress.

3 Read the sentences making excuses and blaming others. Which three are more confrontational?

1 I'd never have deleted it if I'd known you needed it.
2 Don't look at me! It's your job not mine!
3 The thing is, it's not really my job to do that.
4 I wasn't the one who said it was a good idea to do it like that!
5 I'm not trying to get out of it but it's not all my fault.
6 I wasn't the last one to drive the car.

4 Choose the most appropriate phrases for these situations.

1 Your boss wants to know why you didn't sign some important documents.
You say:
    a Don't look at me! I wasn't the one who was supposed to sign them.
    b The thing is, I thought Carlo was doing it.

2 Your housemate is looking for the remote control for the TV. He thinks you have it.
You say:

   a I wasn't the last one to use it. Pete was watching the football earlier.

   b In my defence, I don't watch the TV.

3 You're 30 minutes late to meet a client who's annoyed.
You say:

   a I'm so sorry. I was trying to find somewhere to park.

   b I wasn't the one who suggested meeting somewhere so far away!

Get speaking

 41

 Read the situations and think about what you might say in the conversations below. Then play the audio. Listen and respond when you hear the beeps.

1 A colleague asks about some files that were deleted from a memory stick. You did it accidentally. Admit responsibility.

2 Listen again. This time, try to blame someone else.

3 Listen again. This time, make an excuse that you didn't know it was her memory stick.

4 Your friend is angry that you forgot to buy meat for a barbecue. Blame him for not giving you a list.

5 Listen again. This time, confess that you forgot to take the list.

6 Listen again. This time, make an excuse about why you forgot to buy the meat.

7 Your boss sees you in a café when you're supposed to be at a meeting. You're actually meeting the client there. Explain why you are there.

Everyday language

1

Look at Conversations 1–3 on pages 48–49 again. Find phrases with the meanings below.

Conversation 1

I can't believe ... is necessary again!

Conversation 2

I'm nervous about the result of this!

Conversation 3

I don't know anything about ...

The answers to the exercise above are your Everyday language phrases for this unit. Go to page 90 to see these phrases in context. Then try to use them yourself.

Next steps

TV dramas and soap operas can be a good place to hear people blaming each other, denying things and making excuses. Occasionally, characters even admit responsibility for things too!

Find a show that appeals to you, then listen out for interesting language while you watch.

12 GOSSIPING

Getting started

1 What was the last piece of gossip you heard?
2 Why do you think people are so interested in other people's lives?
3 Do you gossip? What about?

Conversations

42

Read and listen to extracts from four conversations.

Conversation 1

Sally: **Have you heard about Jeff?**

Liam: No, what?

Sally: He's in hospital.

Liam: Oh! Why?

Sally: Stress and overwork, it seems. I think two weeks in bed will do him good. He's been working far too hard.

Liam: Really?

Sally: Yeah. Someone told me he practised presentations in the shower, and I heard he even took a work call in the middle of his daughter's wedding last month!

Liam: Wow! I bet he's finding it hard to adjust to being ill and having to slow down.

Sally: Huh! Hardly! **Apparently**, he's been taking conference calls from his sickbed, and yesterday he persuaded the nurses to send an email for him!

Conversation 2

Martina: Oh, I almost forgot! **You'll never guess what I heard!**

Yolanda: What?

Martina: You know John and Sarah went on holiday last week?

Yolanda: Yeah.

Martina: Well, they got married while they were there!

Yolanda: You're joking!

Martina: No, it's true. His sister told me.

Yolanda:	Well, **I'd never have expected that.** I mean, they've only known each other five minutes. Why do you think they did it like that – I mean, without their families there or anything?
Martina:	Well, **I'm not one to gossip but** I reckon it's because his parents can't stand Sarah.

Conversation 3

Germain:	So somehow he's made everyone think it was his idea! So I went to speak to him about it and I was like, 'I don't think so. I was the one that said it at the meeting.'
Sian:	Too right! And what did he say to that?
Germain:	Oh, he was all defensive and said that, yeah, I was the one that had brought it up at the meeting but it was his idea originally. I couldn't believe it!
Sian:	**Between you and me**, I think he's just worried about his job with all the restructuring the company's doing.
Germain:	Well, maybe. **Don't tell anyone but** Sue told me a while ago that his department is where most of the cuts will be.

Conversation 4

Elsa:	**Guess what!**
Mattias:	What?
Elsa:	Jenny's selling her flat and moving to Kenya!
Mattias:	That's crazy! What about her job? Are you sure?
Elsa:	Yeah. She says she'll find work out there. Says she's fed up with her job and wants a change.
Mattias:	Wow! Kenya's definitely a change! **She's the last person I'd have expected to** do something like that. She's so sensible.
Elsa:	Well, that's what I thought too but I saw her yesterday and she was going, 'I just need a fresh start,' and when I asked what had happened, she just went, 'I don't want to talk about it. I'm leaving and that's it.'
Mattias:	Something big must have happened, then.
Elsa:	I reckon so, because that's a major change of tune.

Language note

Germain and Elsa are both reporting what someone has said to them by quoting the original words. In informal conversation with friends, some people (especially young people) don't use reporting verbs such as *said, told me*, etc. They use phrases such as:

I was like, 'I don't think so.'   *I went, 'You must be joking!'*

Understanding

1 Answer the questions about Conversations 1–4.

1 Who is surprised by the news they hear? ....

2 Who isn't surprised? ....

3 In which two conversations are the speakers talking about something they've heard indirectly? ....

4 Who is recounting something that happened to them personally? ....

2 Look at the bold phrases in Conversations 1–4 and match them to the correct strategies a–c below.

   a Sharing news   **b** Sharing a secret   **c** Reacting to news

3 To which strategies in Exercise 2 would you match the following phrases?

1 Promise not to tell anyone but …   **3** Who would've predicted that?

2 I shouldn't really be saying anything but …

4 Underline all the exclamations that show people reacting to news in Conversations 1–4.

Saying it accurately

1 Complete the sentences with the words from the box.

tell	anything	heard	Between	Promise
last	Apparently	never guess	gossip	expected

1 ...., no one realized it would be so expensive.

2 I'm not one to .... but I heard Fran's in loads of trouble with the bank.

3 Don't .... anyone but I think Mike's about to quit!

4 .... not to tell anyone, but the company's lost that big Pearson's account.

5 .... you and me, she should think herself lucky he didn't find out!

6 Have you .... about Charlie's wedding?

7 I'd never have .... them to split up! They were so in love!

8 You'll .... what I heard! Steve's failed his course!

9 I shouldn't really be saying .... but I think they're far too young to settle down.

10 He's the .... person I'd have expected to drop out of college.

Saying it appropriately

43

1 Listen to two versions of two sentences. Which speaker, a or b, sounds as if they're sharing a secret?

Listen to two versions of another sentence and notice the difference in stress and intonation. Which speaker, a or b, is emphasizing that they've got this gossip secondhand?

 Listen to all the sentences again. Repeat them, copying the stress and intonation.

1 Between you and me, I don't think their business has any chance of success at all!

2 I shouldn't really be saying anything but it looks like he's going to lose his licence.

3 Apparently, she told him he's got one last chance and then it's over!

Get speaking

Read the situations and think about how you could introduce the gossip or react to some news. Then play the audio. Listen and respond when you hear the beeps.

1 You're talking to a friend about a mutual friend, Claire.
 • Start the conversation and introduce the gossip: Claire's moving to Spain next month.
 • Give more information: she met a Spanish man on holiday and is moving to be with him.

2 You're telling a friend something confidential about a mutual friend, Robin.
 • Start the conversation and introduce the gossip: Robin failed all his university exams.
 • Give more information: Robin's been partying every weekend.
 • Give more information: his parents have refused to give him any more money.

3 A friend is telling you surprising news about a mutual friend, a female former CEO. React to the news.

4 A colleague is telling you about a conversation she had with her boss. React to what she says.

Everyday language

Look at Conversations 2–4 on pages 52–53 again. Find phrases with the meanings below.

Conversation 2
They haven't known each other for long.

Conversation 4
That's a big difference in attitude.

Conversation 3
I agree

The answers to the exercise above are your Everyday language phrases for this unit. Go to page 90 to see these phrases in context. Then try to use them yourself.

Next steps

Watch soap operas and reality TV shows like *Big Brother* to hear people sharing gossip.

If you are in an English-speaking country, listen to people talking on the bus – a prime spot for catching up on people's news!

13 HANDLING DIFFICULT CONVERSATIONS

Getting started

1 What kinds of topics can offend people where you're from? Does this differ from other countries?

2 How do you handle a conversation you find offensive?

3 What do you do if someone speaks to you in a way you don't like?

Conversations

46

1 Read and listen to extracts from three conversations.

> ### Conversation 1
>
> **Mark:** ... and what was it you said you did again?
>
> **Noah:** I'm a dentist.
>
> **Mark:** Ah yes, I remember. You earn loads, you dentists, don't you?
>
> **Noah:** Ha ha! Not as much as we're worth!
>
> **Mark:** Ha! But really, how much *do* you earn?
>
> **Noah:** None of your business, mate!
>
> **Mark:** I see, don't want to admit it, eh? Come on, I'm just curious.
>
> **Noah:** Well, **I'd rather not say, actually.**
>
> **Mark:** Oh, I see! I've always wondered why it's so expensive to get anything done to my teeth and it must be the dentist's salary.
>
> **Noah:** Ah ... **Let's change the subject, shall we?** How do you ...
>
> **Mark:** Take me, for example. I earn £50,000 a year and I bet you're on at least twice that.
>
> **Noah:** I wish!
>
> **Mark:** Come on, spill the beans!
>
> **Noah:** Look, **if you don't mind** ... it's not really, I mean ... er ... **I'd really rather not discuss it** so let's leave it there.
>
> **Mark:** Okay then!

> ### Conversation 2
>
> **Lois:** I think they're all really rude!
>
> **Stephanie:** Woah, you can't really generalize ...
>
> **Lois:** I can if it's true! Young people in my day were much better brought up. They're rude *and* they're arrogant.

Stephanie:	Sorry, but **I think that's a bit harsh!**
Lois:	I don't. There are one or two nice teenagers around – your two are lovely, of course, dear – but their friends are quite the hooligans.
Stephanie:	**That's really out of order.** How would you like it if someone was talking about your grandchildren like that?
Lois:	I wouldn't mind if it were true.
Stephanie:	Right, well, **everyone's entitled to their own opinion**, I suppose, but **let's just drop it, shall we?**
Lois:	**Fine.** Whatever you say, dear.
Stephanie:	So **anyway**, there's supposed to be a good film on TV tonight.

Conversation 3

Chuck:	But these don't make any sense at all! Who told you to do reports like this?
Maria:	Er … you did actually.
Chuck:	I doubt that very much. You'll have to redo all of them. There's no way they can go out like that. Honestly, a bit of common sense wouldn't go amiss!
Maria:	Sorry, but **I'd rather you didn't speak to me like that.** You're not my boss. And even if you were, I wouldn't expect …
Chuck:	Yeah, sorry. Pressure's getting to me a bit. Just ignore me.

Cultural note

One way of getting out of conversations you don't want to participate in is to use humour to deflect the other person. In Conversation 1, Noah tries to make a joke to avoid stating his salary. In this case it didn't work and he was forced to be more direct, but often the other person will take your hint.

In English it's common to apologize before saying something direct, rude or potentially shocking for the other person. Stephanie apologizes before disagreeing with Lois in Conversation 2, and Maria apologizes in Conversation 3 before stating quite directly how she feels.

Understanding

1 One speaker in each of Conversations 1–3 was uncomfortable. Match the speakers to the reasons for their discomfort.

1	Noah	**a**	feeling that someone's opinions were inappropriate
2	Stephanie	**b**	finding the conversation too personal
3	Maria	**c**	not liking the way they were being spoken to

2 Look at the bold phrases in Conversations 1–3 and match them to the correct strategies a–c below.

a Avoiding giving an answer

b Changing the subject

c Expressing disapproval

Saying it accurately

1 Match phrases 1–4 to their equivalents a–d.

1 I think that's a bit harsh.
2 That's really out of order.
3 Everyone's entitled to their own opinion.
4 I'd rather you didn't speak to me like that.

a That's one way of looking at it.
b You've got no right to talk to me like that!
c That's going too far.
d I think that's a bit unfair.

Saying it appropriately

47

1 Listen to conversations a and b where speakers try to change the subject. Answer the questions.

1 Which words do the second speakers say slowly? ....
2 Which word does the second speaker in (b) say quickly? ....
3 In both conversations, where does the second speaker pause? ....

2 Listen to the second speakers again and repeat. Copy the tone of voice and intonation.

a Okay then.
b Right. Anyway, …

48

3 Starting a sentence with 'Look, …' can make the next phrase sound firm. Stressing the word makes it even firmer. Listen. Which speakers sound firm because they are not happy with the way the previous speaker is talking?

1 Look, this isn't the right time to talk about it.
2 Look, I'd rather not discuss it if you don't mind.
3 Look, I think you've misunderstood something here.
4 Look, that's not really anything to do with you.

4 Listen again and repeat. Copy the stress to sound firm or more neutral.

> **Language note**
>
> In Conversation 2, Lois says 'Fine. Whatever you say.' This could sound as if she's agreeing but, in fact, she is completely disagreeing but unwilling to argue about it.

5 Read the situations and choose a or b.

1 You're talking to a friend. You've had some health problems recently but are fine now and would rather forget about it.

Friend: So are there any long-term problems? What did the doctor say last time you went?

You:

a If you don't mind, can we change the subject?

b Let's drop it, shall we?

2 The friend carries on pushing the topic and you need to be a bit firmer.

Friend: You can tell me! What are friends for?

You:

a Anyway, … what's on TV later?

b Look, I'd really rather not discuss it.

Get speaking

1 You are having conversations with people who are talking in a way that makes you uncomfortable. Play the audio. Listen and respond when you hear the beeps.

1 You are talking to colleagues at work. (Three conversations: a–c)

2 You are talking to friends. (Three conversations: a–c)

Everyday language

1 Look at Conversations 1–3 on pages 56–57 again. Find phrases with the meanings below.

Conversation 1	**Conversation 2**	**Conversation 3**
Let's look at … as an example.	when I was young	I wish I/we had …!
Tell me the truth!	Think about how you'd feel if …	

The answers to the exercise above are your Everyday language phrases for this unit. Go to page 90 to see these phrases in context. Then try to use them yourself.

Next steps

It's easy to just stay quiet when someone says things you're not happy about, especially in another language. Next time a conversation isn't going the way you'd like it to, try using some of the language from this unit to express how you feel.

---

14 TALKING ABOUT MONEY

Getting started

1 Is it acceptable in your culture to talk about money?
2 In what kinds of situations do you have to talk about money?
3 Are you comfortable offering to pay for something for someone, e.g. a meal?

Conversations

50

1 Read and listen to extracts from three conversations.

Conversation 1

Waiter: That's £20.45, please.

Mario: **This one's on me.**

Kylie: No, no, **I'll get this**, I insist. **I owe you for** the other week anyway. Besides, I just got my annual bonus at work so I'm **feeling quite flush** at the moment!

Mario: Lucky you! If I'd known you were **loaded** I would have ordered dessert! I just had **to fork out for** repairs to my car. That thing **costs me a fortune.**

Kylie: Yeah, I'm glad I got rid of mine when I did or I'd be the same.

Conversation 2

Ingmar: So they offered me that job I went for – like an apprentice kind of thing …

Tamara: Great! Well done!

Ingmar: … but I turned it down.

Tamara: What? Why? I thought you really wanted it.

Ingmar: Yeah – till I heard the salary they're offering. Only £10,000. **I can't live off that!**

Tamara: Yeah, slave wage. Surely no one's going to say yes to that.

Ingmar: I mean, I was on £12,000 in my last job and I was **barely making ends meet** then. There's no way I could do it on ten.

Tamara: The thing that gets me is they're a big fashion house. They must be **rolling in it** but they pay peanuts.

Ingmar: Well, that's it, isn't it? People do it just for the experience.

Conversation 3

Trevor: Yeah, not too bad, thanks. How are things with you? Did Margaret find a job?

Deepak: Not yet, no, so **money's a bit tight** at the moment, but we're managing. What else can you do, eh?

Trevor: Yeah, times are tough, that's for sure.

Deepak: Yep. How about you? You're **doing alright for yourself**, it looks like?

Trevor: Finally, yeah, I am. Beats last year when I was **up to my eyes in debt**!

Deepak: Well, good! Anyway, how are the kids?

Understanding

1 Look at Conversations 1–3 again and answer the questions.

1 Which two speakers say that their financial situation is good at the moment?

....

2 Which speaker's financial situation is not so good at the moment?

....

3 Which speaker is temporarily lacking money? ....

2 Look at the bold phrases in Conversations 1–3 and write them under the correct headings in the table below.

Not having enough money	Having enough or a lot of money
1	1 ....
2	2 ....
3	3 ....
4	4 ....
Talking about spending money	**Offering to pay**
1	1 ....
2	2 ....
	3 ....

Cultural note

Talking about money can be a tricky subject. In a lot of cultures, talking about the prices of things as being high or low is generally acceptable, whereas talking about personal finances is not. A lot of people avoid talking about salaries completely as it can be a very taboo topic (especially in Britain).

Before you start talking about money, take a moment to think about who you're talking to – their nationality, whether you're having a personal or a professional conversation, how old he or she is in relation to you, whether you've talked about money with this person before. All of these factors are important when deciding whether this sort of conversation is appropriate.

Saying it accurately

1 Complete the sentences with the words from the box.

tight	get this	eyes	ends meet
rolling	forking out	live off	flush

1 It's okay. Put your wallet away. I'll ....

2 I feel like I'm constantly .... for some bill or other these days!

3 I'm up to my .... in credit card debt.

4 Do you mind if we stay in tonight? Money's a bit .... at the moment.

5 It's okay, I'm feeling quite .... at the moment. I'll take you out!

6 They're cutting our salaries by 15%. I can't .... that!

7 My brother's just had a huge pay rise, so he's .... in it.

8 It's hard to see other people buying new cars while I'm barely making ....

> **Language note**
>
> *I can't live off that!* has the same meaning as *I can't live on that!*
>
> Phrasal verbs like *live on* and *live off* are a great tool for adding variety to your speech. Invest in a good phrasal verbs dictionary to increase your vocabulary.

Saying it appropriately

51

1 Read the sentences. Underline the words which should be stressed to add emphasis. Then listen and check.

1 I'm up to my eyes in debt.

2 I'm barely making ends meet.

3 I'm rolling in it!

4 That holiday cost me a fortune!

2 Listen again and repeat the sentences. Copy the stress and intonation to add emphasis.

3 Look at these pairs of sentences with similar meanings. Choose the one which is more appropriate if you want to exaggerate.

1 **a** I'm doing alright for myself.   **b** I'm loaded at the moment.

2 **a** I'm rolling in it.   **b** I'm feeling quite flush these days.

3 **a** Money's been a bit tight recently.   **b** I'm barely making ends meet.

4 **a** I'm barely making ends meet.   **b** I'm up to my eyes in debt.

5 **a** It cost me a fortune.   **b** It was expensive.

Speaking tip: exaggeration

We often use exaggeration when we want to be humorous, for example when we are chatting with friends or don't want to be too serious about a situation.

4 Try saying each of these phrases aloud. Make it clear that you are exaggerating, and aim to sound humorous rather than serious.

1 Oh, our boss has a dozen cars and just as many houses. I'm not jealous!

2 Your car cost how much?! What's it made of – gold?

3 It must be their tenth holiday this year. They're never home!

4 I've no money this week. I've got to live off rice until I get paid.

5 It's going to take me the rest of my life to pay this loan off.

Get speaking

 1 Listen to five people making offers or suggestions. Decide if you can afford to do what they suggest, then respond when you hear the beeps.

52

 2 Read the situation and think about what you might say in the conversation below. Listen and respond when you hear the beeps.

53

You are in a restaurant with your friend, Robert.

- Offer to pay.
- Insist on paying because he helped you out with something else recently.

Everyday language

1 Look at Conversations 2–3 on pages 60–61 again. Find phrases with the meanings below.

Conversation 2

I strongly doubt anyone will …
It's impossible that …
The really annoying part about that is …

Conversation 3

Things are difficult for everyone at the moment.

The answers to the exercise above are your Everyday language phrases for this unit. Go to page 91 to see these phrases in context. Then try to use them yourself.

Next steps

Websites and forums talking about personal finance are a good place to find language on this topic. Try www.moneysavingexpert.com. There are also some TV programmes you could watch. Try searching on the Internet for *Bank of Mum & Dad* or financial advice TV shows.

15 TALKING ABOUT STRESS

Getting started

1 Have you had a bad day recently?
2 How does stress affect you?
3 Do you prefer to talk to someone about it or just try and forget it?

Conversations

54

1 Read and listen to extracts from four conversations.

Conversation 1

Alanna: Oh, you've got to be kidding me!

Miles: You okay? What happened?

Alanna: That.

Miles: Oh ... ! Here let me ...

Alanna: Just leave it, okay? I can do it!

Miles: Only trying to help.

Alanna: Well don't!

Miles: Man, **someone got out of bed on the wrong side** this morning.

Alanna: Sorry, it's just **I've had the day from hell** and my boss is being a nightmare and oh – everything! **Things are getting me down.**

Miles: Poor you! Would a cup of tea help?

Alanna: Maybe ... . **I'll snap out of it by tomorrow.**

Miles: Let's hope so or we'll have to buy a new set of plates!

Conversation 2

Cashier: That's twenty-seventeen.

Jerry: Oh no! I think I've left my purse at home. Sorry, **it's really not my day today.**

Cashier: **Happens to us all!**

Jerry: **It's just been one thing after another,** honestly! And that means I haven't got the office keys either. I'll have to go back ... sorry ... can you ... ah, maybe I can come back later?

Cashier: No problem, I can leave it to one side for you.

Jerry: Would you mind? Sorry, again ... **my head's all over the place today.**

Conversation 3

Jaslo:	Hello?
Ilaria:	Hi, it's me. How you doing?
Jaslo:	Oh, yeah, I'm okay. You?
Ilaria:	What's wrong? Something happened?
Jaslo:	Nah … **I'm a bit down today,** that's all.
Ilaria:	Awww. Want to come over for lunch and tell me about it? I was calling to see if you wanted to meet up anyway.
Jaslo:	Er … thanks but **I'm not in the mood for** company.
Ilaria:	Well, if you're sure …
Jaslo:	I wouldn't be very good company, to be honest.
Ilaria:	Okay, then … . Sure you don't want to just pop over for a while?

Conversation 4

Craig:	Argh …! **What is it with me and computers today?** I can't get anything to work!
Magda:	Let me have a look … . Aha! It was that program causing the problem. Just reboot and it should be fine.
Craig:	Thanks. I'll just sit and look at that mountain of paperwork in my in tray while I wait for it to reboot! **I'm completely snowed under** at the minute.
Magda:	Oh yeah? **Anything I can do to help?**
Craig:	No, not really, but thanks anyway. I'll figure it out. **Things are just getting on top of me.**
Madga:	Well, **we've all been there.** If you change your mind, just ask!
Craig:	I will.

Understanding

1 **Match the sentence halves.**

1	Things are getting …	**a**	me and … today?
2	I'm not in the …	**b**	day today.
3	I'm a bit …	**c**	top of me.
4	Everything's getting on …	**d**	snowed under.
5	It's just been one …	**e**	all over the place today.
6	My head's …	**f**	me down.
7	I'll snap out of it …	**g**	down today.
8	It's not my …	**h**	thing after another.
9	What is it with …	**i**	mood for … today.
10	I'm completely …	**j**	by tonight.

2 The phrases below are used to respond to someone who's having a bad day. Complete the phrases with the missing letters.

1 Anything I can do to h_lp?

2 We've all b_ _n th_r_.

3 Someone's got _ _t of b_d on the wr_ng side!

4 H_pp_ns to us _ll!

3 Look at the bold phrases in Conversations 1–4 again. Answer the questions.

1 Which phrase makes a joke out of the person's bad mood?

2 Which phrase suggests things will improve?

3 Which phrase is about a specific thing that's going badly?

Speaking tip: showing support

When someone is having a bad day, you might want to show support. Unit 8 has more phrases for being supportive.

Saying it accurately

1 Complete the phrases with the words from the boxes.

under	out of	on top of	over

1 Someone got .... bed on the wrong side.

2 Everything's getting .... me.

3 My head's all .... the place.

4 I'm completely snowed ....

mood	day	there	snap

5 I'll .... out of it by tonight.

6 I'm not in the .... for socializing today.

7 It's not my .... today!

8 We've all been ....

Saying it appropriately

55

1 Listen to two versions of two phrases. Does speaker a or b sound the most stressed?

2 Listen again to the first speaker. Underline the stressed words.

1 It's just been one thing after another.

2 I'm not in the mood for dealing with this today!

3 Listen again to both versions and repeat. Copy the stress and tone of voice to show how badly your day is going.

Speaking tip: stress and tone of voice

Using different patterns of stress and tone of voice will make people respond differently to you. The angrier and more stressed you sound, the more people will probably try and stay out of your way! Think about how well you know someone before putting everything you feel into the phrases.

Get speaking

1 Read the situations and think about what you might say in the conversations below. Then play the audio. Listen and respond when you hear the beeps.

1 You're in a very bad mood because you've got lots of deadlines to meet.
  - Talk about how stressed you are.
  - Say things will improve later.

2 You've just broken something for the second time today.
  - Say why you are stressed.
  - Give more information about your bad day.

3 You've lost your car keys.
  - Explain why you are stressed.
  - Respond with more information about your bad day.

2 Listen to three stressed people and respond when you hear the beeps.

Everyday language

1 Look at Conversations 2–4 on pages 64–65 again. Find phrases with the meanings below.

Conversation 2	Conversation 3	Conversation 4
I'll put it over here and save it for you.	I am serious about this.	right now
	Come for a short visit.	I'll find the solution.

The answers to the exercise above are your Everyday language phrases for this unit. Go to page 91 to see these phrases in context. Then try to use them yourself.

Next steps

Along with daily situations in soap operas, TV dramas often have characters in stressful situations. Try dramas set in hospitals or police units. *Holby City* and *Casualty* in the UK and *ER* in the US are medical dramas. Police detective series like *Law and Order* have versions in the UK and the US.

16 SHOWING THAT YOU'RE SCEPTICAL

Getting started

1   Do you remember the last thing you heard or read that you didn't believe?

2   Do you find it easy to challenge people about what they're saying?

Conversations

Read and listen to extracts from four conversations.

Conversation 1

Stella: Yeah, it's true. I saw this documentary the other day about how being hungry actually makes you live longer. They had these mice that lived longer when they had their food restricted.

Roger: Mmmm, but **I don't see how it follows that** what happens to mice will happen to people.

Stella: They said there were all kinds of health benefits if you really cut down on what you eat.

Roger: **That doesn't make much sense.** I mean, what about people in poor countries who are really hungry? They don't live longer, do they?

Stella: Oh, I forgot to say you only do it for two days a week – so you eat normally for five days and eat very little for two days. Yeah, and of course it only works if you have a healthy diet as well, with all your nutrients and everything – just *less* of it.

Roger: But why would that make any difference to health?

Stella: It was something to do with the way cells behave when we're hungry, and how people thousands of years ago had to hunt for food so they couldn't just eat whenever they wanted to.

Roger: Hmmm, **I'm not convinced.** I mean, **is there any evidence to back that up?**

Stella: I'm just not explaining very well. You should watch the documentary.

Conversation 2

Glen: I don't really care. I believe that ghosts *do* exist!

Miranda: No, they don't!

Glen: **How can you be so sure?**

Miranda:	How can you? **Where's the proof?**
Glen:	Millions of people have seen ghosts. They can't all be wrong!
Miranda:	Millions of people used to think the Earth was flat. **That argument doesn't hold water** at all.
Glen:	Well, I've seen some pretty strange things myself. And my mom swears she used to see my grandma at the breakfast table every so often, for years after she died. Just you wait, one day you might see something and then you'll have to believe in them.
Miranda:	Well, since ghosts don't exist, **that's hardly likely to happen, is it?**

Conversation 3

Ray:	Cup game Saturday then? Who's going to win, do you reckon?
Craig:	City – easily.
Ray:	Really? **What makes you think that?** They're lucky to have got this far – **there's no chance of** them going all the way to the final.
Craig:	You'll see. I think they've got a real chance, now they've got rid of Carluccio and got Wicks instead. Two nil to City, that's what I think.
Ray:	**I wouldn't put money on it!**

Conversation 4

Mickey:	I know the official line is there's no takeover, but **I'm not buying it.** I know they've been talking to Mottsons. You know, the supermarket.
Rupee:	**Are you sure that's right?**
Mickey:	Ah, well … I know they're having a meeting with them tomorrow.
Rupee:	Having a meeting? Is that it? **That doesn't prove anything!**
Mickey:	It proves they're having talks.
Rupee:	**There could be any number of reasons for** that meeting.
Mickey:	Well, maybe. But why is it happening now then? Something's going on, I'm sure of it.

Understanding

1 Look at the bold phrases in Conversations 1–4. Answer the questions.

1 Which phrases express doubt strongly?

2 Which phrases sound slightly hesitant?

3 Which phrases ask someone to explain their position?

2 Choose the phrase that is stronger.

1 a I wouldn't put money on it.   **b** There's no chance of that happening.

2 a That argument doesn't hold water.   **b** I don't see how it follows that …

3 **a** What makes you think that? **b** Where's the proof?

4 **a** I'm not buying it. **b** Are you sure that's right?

Cultural note

Although the people in the conversations doubt what the other is saying, they are still quite respectful of each other's views. They ask for evidence or further arguments and, even if they remain unconvinced, they don't criticize the other person for their views. Saying things like 'That's rubbish!' or 'You're talking nonsense' might offend people.

Saying it accurately

1 Put the words in the right order to make phrases from Conversations 1–4.

1 That / sense / doesn't / much / make / . ...

2 it / That's / likely / hardly / is / to / happen /, / ? ....

3 I / it / money / on / put / wouldn't / . ...

4 to / there / back / that / any / Is / evidence / up / ? ....

5 water / doesn't / argument / That / hold / . ...

6 any / for / reasons / There / that / of / be / could / number / ! ....

2 Choose the right word to complete each sentence.

1 There's no *chance / opportunity* of Nadal winning Wimbledon again!

2 I'm not *believing / buying* it!

3 I'm not *convinced / convicted*.

4 I don't see how it *follows / figures* that …

5 Where's the *prove / proof*?

6 How can you be so *surely / sure*?

Saying it appropriately

1 Choose the more appropriate option.

1 You are at a formal event, chatting to someone you don't know.

They say: Of course this government isn't going to win the next election.

You say:

a What makes you think that?

b I wouldn't put money on it!

2 You are at work, talking to visitors to your company.

One of them says: Imports are where the big money is so there's no point making your own products any more. There won't be any production in this country in ten years.

You say:

a That's hardly likely to happen, is it?

b I don't see how it follows that a rise in imports means companies will cut production completely.

3 A friend you know well says: I read a theory that they never really landed on the moon. The photos were all faked in a studio.

You say:

a I don't buy it.

b I'm not completely convinced by that.

2 You can use intonation to sound sceptical. Listen to two versions of two conversations. In which conversations, a or b, do the second speakers sound sceptical?

3 Listen again and repeat the sceptical versions of the responses below. Copy the intonation.

1 Mmmm.

2 Mmmm. Really?

Get speaking

1 Read the situations, then play the audio. Listen to different people giving opinions and respond to show you're sceptical when you hear the beeps.

1 You're speaking to a good friend.

2 You're with friends of your friend who you don't know well.

3 You're at work with colleagues who you know but the setting is formal.

4 You're at lunch with colleagues you know well.

5 You're at a party where you have only just met the people you're talking to.

Everyday language

1 Look at Conversations 1–4 on pages 68–69 again. Find phrases with the meanings below.

Conversation 1

It was connected to …

Conversation 2

You're going to see I was right.

Conversation 3

You're going to see I was right.

Conversation 4

Something suspicious is happening.

The answers to the exercise above are your Everyday language phrases for this unit. Go to page 91 to see these phrases in context. Then try to use them yourself.

Next steps

Debates on TV or radio are good places to hear people showing that they're sceptical. Try watching or listening to debates on websites such as the BBC's, and notice how the speakers show that they're sceptical of what other people are saying.

17 SOUNDING CONFIDENT OR HESITANT

Getting started

1   How confident are you in new situations?
2   What kinds of things make you nervous?
3   Are you good at hiding your nerves from other people?

Conversations

61

Read and listen to extracts from three conversations.

Conversation 1

Dan: Your sales figures are great again. Go you!

Sam: Thanks. **All in a day's work**. Actually the boss called me in to congratulate me, and they've given me the big new Anderson account.

Dan: Hey! Way to go! Well done, buddy! Think you can handle it? It's a tough account.

Sam: Yeah. I think so. I **can** do this stuff **in my sleep**. Should be **a piece of cake!**

Conversation 2

Richard: What did the boss want?

Henry: He's given me the big presentation for Smithson's to do.

Richard: Good for you! That's great!

Henry: Yeah. It's good to get the opportunity but I**'m not exactly an expert at** presentations. **It's not** the speaking **that worries me, it's** getting the content right. You know, it's much more up *your* street.

Richard: You'll be fine. It'll be good experience for you.

Henry: Yeah, but I**'m not brilliant with** PowerPoint either. **It's all a bit beyond me,** to be honest.

Richard: Oh, don't worry about that! I'll help. I**'m a whizz with** PowerPoint.

Conversation 3

Liam: So, you've got that job interview tomorrow, right? Feeling good about it?

Cristina: I don't know. I haven't had much time to research the company so I'm feeling kind of unprepared.

Liam:	Ah, come on! You've got loads of experience. You know the industry inside out. **You've got it in the bag!**
Cristina:	Yeah, but I know they have at least two internal candidates so I think **it's not looking good**.
Liam:	Oh, come on. Be positive. Maybe they're looking for someone to bring something fresh to the team.
Cristina:	Hmmm. **I can't see it happening.** But I guess you never know, right?
Liam:	Listen, if they do want someone new, then **you're bound to** get the job.

Cultural note

What can be seen as confidence in one culture can be interpreted as arrogance in another. On the other hand, sounding too hesitant can give the impression that you lack ability.

In general, it's more acceptable to sound very confident when you're talking to a friend or colleague you know well.

Understanding

1 Look at Conversations 1–3 again and answer the questions.

1 Which speakers sound confident about their abilities? ....

2 Who sounds more hesitant and less confident about their ability?

....

3 Who is optimistic about a future outcome? ....

4 Who is pessimistic about a future outcome? ....

2 Look at the bold phrases in Conversations 1–3 and write them under the correct headings in the table below.

Confident about ability	Hesitant about ability	Optimistic or pessimistic about a future outcome
1	1	1 ....
2	2	2 ....
3	3	3 ....
4	4	4 ....

3 Where would you put these phrases in the table above?

1 It's a walk in the park.

2 It's a dead cert!

3 I'm way out of my depth.

4 I can do this standing on my head.

5 I can hold my own.

73

Saying it accurately

1 Match the sentence halves. Then decide if the phrases sound hesitant (H), confident (C) or possibly arrogant (A).

1	I can hold …	**a**	my depth. ……
2	It's a piece of …	**b**	cake. ……
3	All in a day's …	**c**	my own. ……
4	It's a bit …	**d**	beyond me. ……
5	I'm a bit out of …	**e**	my sleep. ……
6	I can do it in …	**f**	work. ……

2 Complete the sentences with the words from the box.

looking	bag	walk	expert	bound	standing	whizz

1 I'll look at your bike for you. I'm a bit of a .... with bikes.

2 I can't see we'll have any problems. Should be a .... in the park!

3 Yeah, no problem. I can do it .... on my head.

4 Well, I can try and install it for you, but I'm not exactly an .... with computers.

5 We're still waiting to hear if we've got the contract, but it's not .... good.

6 Your ideas were great. You're .... to get the contract.

7 Don't worry. Your proposal was solid. That contract's in the ....

Saying it appropriately

1 Choose the appropriate answer in the following situations. Sometimes more than one answer is possible.

1 Your boss asks you if you're any good at creating spreadsheets in Excel.

You say:

   a Piece of cake!   **b** I can hold my own.   **c** Okay, but I'm a bit out of my depth with formulas and data.

2 A friend asks you for help because they failed their maths exam. You are quite good (but not brilliant) at maths so you say:

   a Sure, I'm a whizz at maths.

   b I'm not exactly an expert but I'll try.

   c Why not? Maths is a walk in the park for me.

3 Your friend asks if you think your team can win a quiz you're going to take part in. You're quite confident, so you say:

   a I can't see it happening.

   b I think we can hold our own.

   c Are you joking? We're a dead cert!

2 Listen to two versions of a conversation. Do the second speakers in each version sound confident or hesitant?

3 Listen again and repeat the responses below. Copy the stress and intonation to sound hesitant or confident.

1 Er … yeah … maybe. I'll give it a go.

2 Er … yeah … maybe. I'll give it a go!

Get speaking

63

1 Read the situations and think about how you could sound confident or hesitant. Then play the audio. Listen and respond when you hear the beeps.

1 You play for a sports team and you have a big match today. You're talking to a teammate who's worried because she thinks the other team are strong competition.
- Express confidence in your team's abilities.
- Express optimism about the outcome of the game.

2 Listen to another teammate. This time, you're not so confident that you can win.
- Express hesitancy about your team's abilities.
- Give a pessimistic view of the outcome of the game.

3 You're talking to your tutor about an important IT exam you have this afternoon. You've studied a lot and it's your best subject.
- Express confidence in your abilities.
- Say it's going to be easy.

4 This time you're talking to your tutor about a maths exam. Maths isn't your best subject, and you don't feel very confident.
- Express hesitancy about your abilities.
- Say you've studied, but you're pessimistic about the outcome.

Everyday language

1 Look at Conversations 1–3 on pages 72–73 again. Find phrases with the meanings below.

Conversation 1

Congratulations!

Conversation 2

Well done!

… is something you know well or are good at.

Conversation 3

You know a lot about … .

The answers to the exercise above are your Everyday language phrases for this unit. Go to page 91 to see these phrases in context. Then try to use them yourself.

Next steps

Watch films and TV shows for ideas on how confident people sound according to their job or social group.

Remember that you are allowed to sound confident even if you don't feel it! Perhaps acting as if you're confident and using appropriate language will help you to feel more confident!

18 SOUNDING EXCITED

Getting started

1 When was the last time you were really excited about something?
2 Who did you tell?
3 What's the best reaction you've had from someone you gave good news to?

Conversations

64

1 Read and listen to extracts from four conversations.

Conversation 1

Ling: Argh, I've been sitting here pressing *Refresh* for an hour!

Jo: Yeah? Why?

Ling: I'm waiting for my exam results. **I wish** they'**d hurry up and** post them … . Oh God, they're up, they're up! Oooooh.

Jo: Well, come on then, what does it say?

Ling: **I can't believe it!** I've got a first!

Jo: Oh! **Congratulations! That's the best news ever!** All those hours in the library really paid off, right?

Ling: Yeah, they definitely did! **I can't wait to tell** my mum! A first!

Conversation 2

Barry: Hi, Mum.

Mum: Hi, darling. How did the interview go? Tell me everything!

Barry: I got it! They offered me the job on the spot!

Mum: Hey! Congratulations! **I'm so excited for you!** Well done! **You must be over the moon!**

Barry: Yeah, it's amazing. **I'm still pinching myself!** This is amazing!

Mum: Well, **I couldn't be happier for you,** darling. I'm really proud of you. Do you want to tell your dad yourself?

Conversation 3

Lydia: What are you doing for Christmas and New Year this year?

Dylan: Christmas with my parents, then we're going skiing in France, actually. Just the two of us.

Lydia:	Ah, recovering from a crazy family Christmas with some alone time, eh?
Dylan:	Yep. **I'm really looking forward to** a change of scenery. We've not been away by ourselves since the twins were born.
Lydia:	Well then, it's about time! Your first grown-up holiday in two years! Who's taking care of them while you're away?
Dylan:	Sarah's parents. They're **dying to** do the whole Christmas thing with their grandkids – they're really excited.

Conversation 4

Marwan:	Hey, I heard your big news. Congratulations! That's amazing!
Britney:	I know!
Marwan:	All those times you see it in the papers and now I can say I know a real live lottery winner. How does it feel?
Britney:	**It hasn't really sunk in yet** but of course **I'm thrilled to bits!**

Language note

It is common to exaggerate when you're excited about something. In Conversation 1, Jo congratulates Ling by saying that it's *the best news ever*. Other phrases which express exaggerated feelings are: *be over the moon* and *be dying to do something*.

Understanding

1 Look at the bold phrases in Conversations 1–4 and write them in the correct sections of the table below.

Sounding excited about something that's happening now	1	....
	2	....
	3	....
	4	....
Sounding excited about something that's happening in the future	1	....
	2	....
	3	....
	4	....
Sounding excited for someone else	1	....
	2	....
	3	....
	4	....

Saying it accurately

1 Match the halves.

1	I can't …	**a**	happier for you!
2	I wish … would …	**b**	news ever!
3	I'm dying …	**c**	wait to tell …
4	I'm thrilled to …	**d**	bits.
5	You must be …	**e**	over the moon!
6	I couldn't be …	**f**	sunk in yet.
7	That's the best …	**g**	forward to …
8	It hasn't really …	**h**	to …
9	I'm looking …	**i**	hurry up and …

Cultural note

You might notice a difference between Americans and British people when they're reacting to good news. British people will often sound less excited than Americans, especially if they don't know you well. As a result, they may be more comfortable with a mid-level excited response to their own good news.

2 Complete the phrases with the correct pronouns.

1 I'm still pinching ....

2 I'm so excited for .... !

3 I can't believe .... !

4 I can't tell .... how pleased I am!

5 .... won't believe what's happened.

6 I'm so pleased to hear ....

Saying it appropriately

1 Listen to six people reacting to some news. Which speakers sound excited? Which sound unexcited?

1 ....   **3** ....   **5** ....

2 ....   **4** ....   **6** ....

2 Listen to the same phrases, all excited this time. Repeat and copy the intonation to sound excited.

1 I'm dying to try that new Mexican place.

2 That's the best news ever.

3 You must be over the moon.

4 I'm still pinching myself.

5 I can't believe it.

6 I wish he'd hurry up and come.

3 Choose two phrases from the box that are appropriate for each situation.

You must be thrilled to bits.	You must be pinching yourself.
I can't wait to go!	I'm really looking forward to it.
I'm over the moon!	I'm thrilled to bits.

1 Your friend has won a competition.

....

....

2 You're moving to a new country next month.

....

....

3 You've just got news that you've been chosen to be on a sports team in your town.

....

....

Get speaking

67

1 Play the audio. Listen to seven short one-sided conversations and think about what you could say in the gaps. Then listen again and respond when you hear the beeps.

Everyday language

1 Look at Conversations 1–4 on pages 76–77 again. Find phrases with the meanings below.

Conversation 1

... was a lot of work but it was worth it.

Conversation 3

somewhere different for a nice change

It's overdue and you deserve it.

a big situation or event

Conversation 4

a genuine ...

The answers to the exercise above are your Everyday language phrases for this unit. Go to pages 91–92 to see these phrases in context. Then try to use them yourself.

Next steps

News coverage of big sporting events or awards ceremonies, e.g. The Oscars, The Grammys, The Brits, can be a good place to hear people sounding excited. Often the interviews are really short sound-bites just before or just after the event, so you can hear lots of different people.

19 SHOWING ANNOYANCE AND ANGER

Getting started

1 What kinds of things make you angry?
2 How acceptable is it to show anger in your culture?
3 How does your language and tone of voice change depending on who you're angry with?

Conversations

 Read and listen to extracts from four conversations.

Conversation 1

Announcer: … train is delayed by thirty minutes.

Corey: **I don't believe it!** Again? **This is absolutely outrageous!** That's the third time this week.

Lewis: Yeah, the trains are **driving me crazy**. It's not as if it's cheap to travel by train!

Corey: I know! I'm going to start cycling to work again. Save myself a fortune …

Announcer: The delayed 17.50 to Crewe has been cancelled due to …

Corey: That's it! **I've had it up to here with** commuting. I'm going to complain!

Lewis: Oh yeah? Who to?

Corey: Someone! Anyone!

Conversation 2

Bobbie: She's given me, like, ten extra things to do just because I'm having next week off.

Shona: Yeah, your boss sucks.

Bobbie: **I'm sick of** the way she dumps all this last-minute stuff on me.
[Phone rings.]
That'll be her. Hello …Yes, hi, Barbara … I'm just on my way back … yeah, sure thing. Great. Now she's got some filing she needs doing 'urgently'.

Shona: **Just take a deep breath** and remember you'll be on a beach this time tomorrow.

Conversation 3

Hugh: Argh! **This is the last thing I need!** This road's closed as well, which means we need to go back to the motorway and take the …

Colleen: We're never going to make it now!

Hugh: Don't you start!

Colleen: I did tell you to bring the satnav …

Hugh: I checked the route online before we left.

Colleen: Which told us the roads were clear two hours ago – very useful. The satnav would have told us …

Hugh: Will you shut up about the stupid satnav? Your constant complaining's **really getting on my nerves**.

Colleen: Okay, okay, **keep your hair on!** Let's just get a map and work out …

Conversation 4

Charlotte: Oh! Look at the state of this place again. **Why can't he just** clear up after himself **for once?**

Dean: How are we supposed to cook in this? There's not a single clean plate!

Charlotte: **It's really bugging me** now! How many times do we have to tell him? Three people live here, not just him. I'm going to have to say something. He makes more of an effort, or we move out.

Dean: **Steady on!** It bugs me too, but you can't go making a big thing of it. It *is* his house.

Charlotte: Yeah, and we pay rent! Oh, look! My milk's gone too. **This is the last straw!**

Dean: Charlotte, chill out! I'll wash up! **Just count to ten** and remember this is the cheapest place we found and we've only got …

Understanding

1   Find a speaker in Conversations 1–4 who is angry about the things below.

1   an untidy flatmate ....

2   a problem on the road ....

3   public transport ....

4   their boss ....

2   Most of the bold phrases in Conversations 1–4 are for expressing annoyance or anger. Which four phrases are for calming someone down?

3   Look at the phrases for expressing anger and annoyance again. Which three express the strongest anger?

Saying it accurately

1 Complete the sentences with the words from the box.

1 This is the last .... I need!
2 Right, that's the last .... !
3 I've had it .... to here with this job!
4 I don't .... it!
5 Just .... to ten and chill out.
6 This is really .... me now!
7 Take a deep .... and remember it's Friday tomorrow!
8 Keep your .... on!
9 He's getting on my .... !
10 .... on!

straw
bugging
nerves
breath
up
steady
count
thing
hair
believe

2 Choose the correct adverb to make the phrases stronger. Sometimes both adverbs are possible.

1 I'm *absolutely* / *very* sick of seeing the neighbour's cat in our garden every day!
2 The trains are *really* / *completely* driving me crazy.
3 This Internet connection is driving me *very* / *totally* crazy.
4 These prices are *absolutely* / *completely* outrageous.
5 He's *very* / *really* bugging me!

Saying it appropriately

69

1 Tone of voice is very important for showing how angry you are. Listen and decide whether each speaker (1–6) sounds calm or angry.

70

2 Read and listen to the same sentences, the speakers all sounding angry this time, and repeat. Copy the tone of voice to sound angry.

1 This is the last thing I need!
2 Sondra's driving me crazy at the moment.
3 I'm sick of hearing about their wedding!
4 Why can't she just mind her own business for once?
5 I've had it up to here with this machine!
6 Right, that's the last straw!

Listen to the same speakers, now all sounding calmer, and repeat. Copy the intonation to sound calm.

71

Cultural note

Look at the difference between 'I'm sick of always arriving everywhere late' (anger at a situation) and 'I'm sick of you always making us late' (anger at a person). Remember that anger at situations rather than people might be more acceptable in some cultures.

Get speaking

 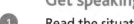 Read the situations and listen to the prompts. Respond when you hear the beeps and show that you are slightly annoyed.

72

1 You're waiting at the airport to fly to Cairo.

2 You're listening to the weather forecast on TV and making plans for the bank holiday weekend.

3 You're driving across the country.

4 You're queuing at an ATM to get money out.

5 You're about to make a cup of tea at home, and your flatmate admits something.

2 Listen again and respond to show that you are very angry.

 3 Listen to two people who are angry. Respond when you hear the beep and try to calm them down

73

Everyday language

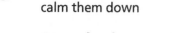 Look at Conversations 1–4 on pages 80–81 again. Find phrases with the meanings below.

Conversation 1

I wouldn't mind as much if ...

Conversation 3

Stop talking about ... (impolitely)

Conversation 4

What a mess ... is!

It's almost impossible for us to ...

The answers to the exercise above are your Everyday language phrases for this unit. Go to page 92 to see these phrases in context. Then try to use them yourself.

Next steps

TV soap operas and dramas are a good place to hear people expressing annoyance and anger. Also try searching for videos or recordings online of real people losing their temper.

20 USING SARCASM

Getting started

1 Do you find sarcasm funny or rude, or both?
2 Have you ever tried to use it?
3 Which countries and cultures use sarcasm the most?

Conversations

74

1 Read and listen to extracts from four conversations.

Conversation 1

Garth: **Oh fantastic! What perfect weather for a day at the beach.**

Pia: Yeah, **I'm so glad we came today instead of yesterday** when it was sunny or we'd have missed this.

Garth: Right, and tomorrow it's going to be lovely so **it's lucky we're back at work**.

Conversation 2

Jenny: Oh, look, is that your Mum over there?

Anthony: No, **it's the Queen.**

Jenny: Ha ha! **Very funny!** I can't see properly without my glasses. I was just checking.

Conversation 3

Dee: Did you know: cherries are a natural cure for headaches. I read it on the Internet somewhere.

Alistair: **Oh well, if you read it on the Internet, it must be true.**

Dee: **Alright, Mr Negative!** I'm just trying to help. Let's see ... cherries ... pain relief. Oh, yeah ... there's something here. See? Told you!

Alistair: Let me see. **Oh, very practical.** You need to eat half your body weight in cherries to get any effect. The drug companies must be terrified.

Conversation 4

Paul: Can you slow down? We're not in Formula 1 here!

Debbie: Oh, **look who's suddenly the road safety expert!** How many times did you get caught speeding last year?

Paul: Exactly. Two speeding tickets makes you an expert! **Just a couple of miles under the speed of light would still get us there on time,** you know.

Debbie: Twenty miles an hour. Is that better for you?

Speaking tip: sarcasm

Sarcasm is an ironic comment that can be used to make a joke or to hurt someone. It is common in humour and is an example of what researchers call *unplain speaking* where what is said is different from its meaning.

Understanding

1 Match the sarcastic (unplain-speaking) phrases with the plain-speaking phrases on the right.

1	It's the Queen.	**a**	If you go a bit slower, we'll still arrive on time.
2	I'm so glad we came today instead of yesterday.	**b**	Not everything on the Internet is true.
3	Look who's suddenly the road safety expert!	**c**	I wish we'd come yesterday instead.
4	It's lucky we're back at work.	**d**	Of course it's my mum!
5	Just a couple of miles under the speed of light would still get us there on time	**e**	The drug companies won't be worried.
		f	You don't know more than me about driving safely!
6	Oh well, if you read it on the Internet, it must be true.	**g**	It's a pity we have to work.
7	The drug companies must be terrified.		

Saying it accurately

1 Complete the sentences with the words from the box.

well	suddenly	Miss	expert	true	must	very

1 Look who's .... the fitness .... !

2 Alright, ... Health Freak!

3 Oh .... , if you read it in the paper, it .... be .... !

4 Oh, ... funny!

Language note

A common type of sarcasm is saying the opposite of what you mean, or the opposite of the truth. Garth says it's lucky they are at the beach on a rainy day. Of course he means the exact opposite. Alistair says 'Oh, very practical' and 'The drugs companies must be terrified' when actually he means that eating a lot of cherries for pain relief is highly impractical and that the drugs companies don't have any reason to worry about losing customers.

2 Which responses are sarcastic?

1 **Pat:** They got back off their holiday to find the neighbour had let the dogs sleep in their bed!

    Angie: **a** They must have been furious.   **b** They must have been thrilled.

2 **Max:** I thought we could just have the same theme for the office party as last year.

    Denise: **a** Oh, very creative.   **b** Oh, very practical.

Speaking tip: exaggeration

Exaggeration is one of the key features of sarcasm. For example, in Conversation 4 Paul compares Debbie's driving to Formula 1 and the speed of light but of course she wasn't really driving at those high speeds.

3 Choose the most sarcastic way of adding to these sentences.

1 Can you give me a bigger piece of cake, please?

   a It's tiny!   **b** I'll need a microscope to find that!

2 When was the last time you tidied your room?

   a Weeks ago?   **b** When man landed on the moon?

3 You're not the worst cook, are you, dear?

   a Only three people died last time   **b** It's getting better anyway.
you made dinner.

Saying it appropriately

1 Listen to two versions of three phrases. Which speakers, a or b, are using a sarcastic tone of voice?

2 Listen again and repeat the sarcastic phrases. Copy the intonation.

  1 No really. I'm having the time   **2** Oh, very helpful!
of my life!   **3** He must be ecstatic!

3 Which response would be most appropriate in the following situations? Could you say both?

  1 You're talking to your boss.

     He says: Can you get that report to me by lunchtime, please?

You say:

a Only if they've invented time machines!　　**b** I'll need more time than that, I'm afraid.

2 You're talking to your teacher.

She says: You're getting much better marks recently. Well done!

You say:

a Thanks, I've been studying a lot.

b Thanks, I live in the library these days. I only leave to get sunlight every now and then.

3 You're talking to a good friend.

He says: Hey, I haven't seen you for ages! I thought you'd left the country or something!

You say:

a Yeah, I've been really busy with work.　　**b** No, I was just avoiding you!

Get speaking

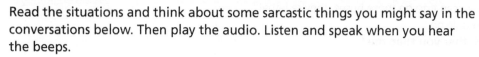

76

Read the situations and think about some sarcastic things you might say in the conversations below. Then play the audio. Listen and speak when you hear the beeps.

1 You're at a picnic and it's just starting to rain. Try saying the opposite of what you mean.

2 You're eating in a restaurant and the food arrives and it's cold. Try exaggerating.

3 You're trying to study, but your housemate's music is too loud.

- Start the conversation and ask your housemate to turn down the music.

- Say something sarcastic and try exaggerating.

4 Your friend is telling you about the latest fashion in shoes, which you think is ridiculous. Try using some of the phrases from *Saying it accurately* Exercise 1.

Listen again and try a different way of being sarcastic for each conversation.

Everyday language

Look at Conversation 3 on page 84 again. Find phrases with the meanings below.

Conversation 3

I'm going to tell you something interesting.
I was right!

The answers to the exercise above are your Everyday language phrases for this unit. Go to page 92 to see these phrases in context. Then try to use them yourself.

Next steps

Sarcasm is a key part of comedy. Find some of the following examples on the Internet or on DVD: *Blackadder* and *Fawlty Towers* (search online for 'Fawlty Towers view of Torquay'), *Friends*, (Chandler is often sarcastic). Professor Snape in the *Harry Potter* films has an extremely sarcastic tone of voice.

EVERYDAY LANGUAGE IN USE

Below are all of the *Everyday language* phrases you saw in the units, each used in one or more real English situation. These examples are all taken from the Collins Corpus, ensuring that they are completely authentic uses of English today.

Unit 1   Bumping into people

- You **were in the middle of** saying something?
- **I'd hate to be in their shoes** having to make that decision.
- I am **sticking to** my views and I will not change them.
- 'You can't go on those buses, they're lethal.'
  'People do.'
  'Rather you than me.'
- 'I refuse to get involved with him.'
  'I don't blame you.'

Unit 2   Talking about yourself

- **You must be joking**. I'm not paying quarter of a million pounds for a house.
- I'm 25, have a successful career and lots of friends but **underneath it all** I'm very lonely.
- 'They said it was going to rain today. And tomorrow morning.'
  'And **since when do you** believe the weather forecast?'
- Most of us would **think twice about** spending so much money on a meal.
- The girls are very interesting, they're very good to talk to. **Seriously now**, I promise!

Unit 3   Telephone and communication problems

- Fine, Joe. I can hear you **loud and clear**.
- The message has been given **loud and clear** to various agencies that there are people in need.
- Talk it over **at your end** and call me back.
- Hello? Donna? **Are you there**?

Unit 4   Exchanging information

- I'm afraid that **when the time comes** I will let them down.
- If you don't win, **there's always** next year, isn't there?
- **If you need any help with** the arrangements, **just let me know**.
- Rail travellers who try to avoid paying their train fares could face **on-the-spot** fines.
- The policeman arrested the man **on the spot**.

Unit 5   Negotiating

- I helped you, you helped me. Now **we're quits**.
- **While we're on the subject** of apologies, I'm sorry I didn't write to you when your wife died.
- The mother works selling drinks and **bits and bobs** in the street.
- **Like I said**, it's his decision, it's his conscience and he's got to live with it.
- 'It's cheap. Five hundred pounds.'
  'You call that cheap. **I was thinking more like** two hundred.'

Unit 6   Interrupting and letting others speak

- I still had two **weeks to go** before the baby was due and I hadn't even packed my hospital bag.
- Flowers? **How** thoughtful **of you**!
- Young people are absorbing new technology much faster than other groups. **Which brings us to** schools …
- You **can't argue with** this result because we defended well as a team.
- Bad weather caused delay and cancellation of scores of flights **to and from** UK airports.
- The team has been winning a few things **in the meantime**, and that's what fans want.

Unit 7   Showing interest

- The pressure of politics is **enough to make anyone** crack. Could you handle it?
- There's little or no access through for pedestrians **let alone** mothers with prams or pushchairs.
- It is difficult to tell what the argument is about, **let alone** how it will be resolved.
- I give them help and advice. After all, **that's what** friends **are for**.
- I can give you some change **if it's any help**.
- It's not enough to say I'm sorry. **If it's any help** I bitterly regret what I did.

Unit 8   Being supportive

- There's a list of questions about **as long as my arm**.
- **I know it sounds stupid but** I didn't realize what I was doing.
- Normally, if you have a back problem, you know about it the moment you do it, but it's something that has **just crept up on me**.
- We are absolutely **flat out with** buyer inquiries and sales.
- I thought I'd be spending my retirement watching TV. Boy was I wrong! I **barely have a minute to myself**.

Unit 9   Persuasion

- It's been lovely talking to you, **as always**.
- The attraction, **as always**, is money.

- I ended up going along with her. Why? Well, partly because I'm such a **pushover**.
- I could **see** the photographer **eyeing up** the Porsche for the return trip.
- Well, **that's settled then**. I'll book the accommodation and you two sort out the travel arrangements.

Unit 10   Being tactful

- Why waste valuable time **slaving in the kitchen**?
- It's no-fuss food and great if you're **watching the old waistline**.
- He is **not the first person to** claim that tides trigger earthquakes.
- 'I am interested …'
  'I can feel a 'but' coming.'
- 'I've got to have lots of things to stop myself from brooding too much.'
  'Such as?'

Unit 11   Admitting and denying

- 'And you're sure you're comfortable with it?'
  'How many times do I have to tell you, Mike**?** I trust your judgement.'
- I'm starting my new job tomorrow. **Wish me luck!**
- I've got to be honest with you. I **haven't got a clue** how to run a youth group

---

Unit 12   Gossiping

- People kept claiming we were madly in love when we'd **only known each other five minutes**.
- 'This is not the kind of guy I want to be the President of the United States.'
  'Too right!'
- **That's a change of tune** as he said two years ago that he would no longer invest in companies that develop drugs.

Unit 13   Handling difficult conversations

- There are people who just laze around. **Take** Martin, **for example**, he can sit in front of the telly all day.
- Arthur was very loyal to Kennedy. He wouldn't go out and **spill the beans**.
- Married women didn't go out to work **in my day**.
- **In my day** every law student became a solicitor or a barrister. Now a whole range of opportunities has opened up.
- **How would you like it if** a camera crew was there to record your reaction to all the changes?
- **How would she like it if** you started talking to her like that?
- A bit of help and advice **wouldn't go amiss**.

Unit 14   Talking about money

- **Surely no one's going to** sit there listening to a fire alarm going off for 20 minutes?
- **There's no way** I'm going to allow my kids to go to this concert.
- **The thing that gets me is** when people spend that much on a bike that they're just going to use for road commuting.
- **Times are tough** right now, but I am incredibly optimistic about the future of this country.

Unit 15   Talking about stress

- Toss the prawns with the garlic, lime zest and sugar, and then **leave** them **to one side** for ten minutes.
- Let's **leave** the detail **to one side**— because the bigger picture is the one that matters most.
- I don't know what's going to happen, **to be honest**.
- I live a fair distance away but may well try and **pop over for a while**.
- It's much more effective than the system we have **at the minute**.
- Don't tell them. They'll **figure it out** one day.

Unit 16   Showing that you're sceptical

- I don't know how to work these things too well but I know it's **something to do with** pulling back the hammer.
- If you think these men look grotty now, **just you wait** till 11 o'clock!
- **You'll see,** Paddy, she'll be here tomorrow telling you she's got to go.
- We had 500 seals dying along the East Coast that year. So **something's going on** there.

Unit 17   Sounding confident or hesitant

- I think Pat should be commended for what he said. **Way to go**, Pat!
- 'I told them that I wouldn't pay £2 for a bit of paper.'
  'Good for you!'
- If you fancy using your IT skills for a worthy cause, then this new scheme could be right **up your street**.
- **I know** this trade **inside out**. I've been in it over 30 years.

Unit 18   Sounding excited

- **All that** hard work has **really paid off**.
- This year we spent a lot on advertising and **it really paid off**.
- You've been through a lot. Maybe it's time for **a change of scenery**.
- It's **about time** politicians in this country started realizing that we don't want this sort of thing.
- **The whole** quality **thing** is crucial to the process.

- I'm not sure there are good alternatives to training medical students on **real live** patients.
- Police officers were dispatched to the scene, where, sure enough, they discovered a **real live** roaring lion.

Unit 19   Showing annoyance and anger

- It's probably unfair of me to comment because **it's not as if** I work for them.
- **It's not as if** I wanted to go out every evening, just weekends.
- OK … now **will you shut up about** the economy being so bad?
- Her hair wants cutting. **Look at the state of** it! Are you any good with scissors?
- **How am I supposed to** do it when I am not even there?
- **How are we supposed to** know this?

Unit 20   Using sarcasm

- **Did you know** Vienna's got more council houses than any other city?
- **Did you know** that a five-minute shower costs an average of only five pence a time?
- 'Maybe I'm not smarter than I look.' **'Told you!'** Judy said.

MINI-DICTIONARY

 Some of the most difficult words from the units are defined here in this mini-dictionary. The definitions are extracts from the Collins COBUILD Advanced Dictionary and focus on the meanings of the words in the contexts in which they appear in the book.

Unit 1

acquaintance N-COUNT an **acquaintance** is someone who you have met and know slightly, but not well. • *The proprietor was an old acquaintance of his.*

bump into PHRASAL VERB If you **bump into** someone you know, you meet them unexpectedly. [INFORMAL] • *I happened to bump into Mervyn Johns in the hallway.*

Unit 3

breakdown N-COUNT The **breakdown** of something such as a relationship, plan, or discussion is its failure or ending. • ... the *breakdown of talks between the US and EU officials.*

Unit 4

digest VERB If you **digest** information, you think about it carefully so that you understand it. • *All this has upset me. I need time to digest it all.*

Unit 5

firm ADJ If you describe someone as **firm**, you mean they behave in a way that shows that they are not going to change their mind, or that they are the person who is in control. • *She had to be firm with him. 'I don't want to see you again.'*

negotiate VERB If people **negotiate** with each other or negotiate an agreement, they talk about a problem or a situation such as a business arrangement in order to solve the problem or complete the arrangement. • *His publishing house had just begun negotiating for her next books.*

tentative ADJ If someone is **tentative**, they are cautious and not very confident because they are uncertain or afraid. • *My first attempts at complaining were rather tentative.*

Unit 6

interrupt VERB If you **interrupt** someone who is speaking, you say or do something that causes them to stop. • *Turkin tapped him on the shoulder. 'Sorry to interrupt, Colonel.'*

Unit 7

echo VERB If you **echo** someone's words, you repeat them or express agreement with their attitude or opinion. • *'That was a truly delicious meal,' he said. 'Yes, wasn't it?' echoed Penelope*

exclamation NOUN An **exclamation** is a sound, word, or sentence that is spoken suddenly, loudly, or emphatically and that expresses excitement, admiration, shock, or anger. • *Sue gave an exclamation as we got a clear sight of the house.*

sincere ADJ If you say that someone is **sincere**, you approve of them because they really mean the things they say. • *'I'm sorry,' he said, sounding sincere.*

synonym N-COUNT A **synonym** is a word or expression which means the same as another word or expression. • *The term 'industrial democracy' is often used as a synonym for worker participation.*

Unit 8

cheer up PHRASAL VERB When you **cheer up** or when something cheers you up, you stop feeling depressed and become more cheerful. • *I think he misses her terribly. You might cheer him up.*

support N-UNCOUNT If you give **support** to someone during a difficult or unhappy time, you are kind to them and help them. • *It was hard to come to terms with her death after all the support she gave to me and the family.*

Unit 9

forceful ADJ If you describe someone as **forceful**, you approve of them because they express their opinions and wishes in a strong, emphatic, and confident way. • *He was a man of forceful character, with considerable insight and diplomatic skills.*

give in PHRASAL VERB If you **give in**, you admit that you are defeated or that you cannot do something. • *All right. I give in. What did you do with the ship?*

persuade VERB If you **persuade** someone to do something, you cause them to do it by giving them good reasons for doing it. • *My husband persuaded me to come.*

reluctant ADJ If you are **reluctant** to do something, you are unwilling to do it and hesitate before doing it, or do it slowly and without enthusiasm. • *Mr Spero was reluctant to ask for help.* **reluctantly** ADV • *We have reluctantly agreed to let him go.*

Unit 10

downplay VERB If you **downplay** a fact or feature, you try to make people think that it is less important or serious than it really is. • *The government is trying to downplay the violence.*

emphasize VERB To **emphasize** something means to indicate that it is particularly important or true, or to draw special attention to it. • *But it's also been emphasized that no major policy changes can be expected to come out of the meeting.*

tactful ADJ If you describe a person or what they say as **tactful** you approve of them because they are careful not to offend or upset another person. • *He had been extremely tactful in dealing with the financial question.*

Unit 11

admit VERB If you **admit** that something bad, unpleasant, or embarrassing is true, you agree, often unwillingly, that it is true. • *I am willing to admit that I do make mistakes.*

blame VERB If you **blame** a person or thing for something bad, you believe or say that they are responsible for it or that they caused it. • *If it wasn't Sam's fault, why was I blaming him?*

deny VERB When you **deny** something, you state that it is not true. • *She denied both accusations.*

fault N-SING If a bad or undesirable situation is your **fault**, you caused it or are responsible for it. • *There was no escaping the fact: it was all his fault.*

Unit 12

gossip VERB If you **gossip** with someone, you talk informally, especially about other people or local events. You can also say that two people gossip. • *Mrs Lilywhite never gossiped.*

gossip N-VAR **Gossip** is informal conversation, often about other people's private affairs. • *There has been much gossip about the possible reasons for his absence.*

Unit 13

harsh ADJ **Harsh** actions or speech are unkind and show no understanding or sympathy. • *He said many harsh and unkind things about his opponents.*

Unit 14

exaggerate VERB If you **exaggerate**, you indicate that something is, for example, worse or more important than it really is. • *Sheila admitted that she did sometimes exaggerate the demands of her job.*

insist VERB If you **insist** that something should be done, you say so very firmly and refuse to give in about it. • *My family insisted that I should not give in, but stay and fight.*

insist on VERB If you **insist on** something, you say firmly that it must be done or provided. • *She insisted on being present at all the interviews.*

owe VERB If you **owe** money to someone, they have paid for something for you, and you have not yet paid the money back to them. You can also say that the money is owing. • *How much do I owe you for the train tickets?*

taboo N-COUNT If there is a **taboo** on a subject or activity, it is a social custom to avoid doing that activity or talking about that subject, because people find them embarrassing or offensive. • *The topic of addiction remains something of a taboo.* **taboo** ADJ is also an adjective. • *Cancer is a taboo subject and people are frightened or embarrassed to talk openly about it.*

Unit 16

argument N-VAR An **argument** is a statement or set of statements that you use in order to try to convince people that your opinion about something is correct. • *There's a strong argument for lowering the price.*

criticize VERB If you **criticize** someone or something, you express your disapproval of them by saying what you think is wrong with them. • *His mother had rarely criticized him or any of her children.*

doubt NOUN Doubt is a feeling of uncertainty about something and not knowing whether it is true or possible. • *Hilton expressed doubt that e-learning would ever overtake face-to-face training.*

doubt VERB If you **doubt** someone or **doubt** their word, you think that they may not be telling the truth. • *No one directly involved with the case doubted him.*

proof N-VAR **Proof** is a fact, argument, or piece of evidence which shows that something is definitely true or definitely exists. • *This is not necessarily proof that he is wrong.*

sceptical ADJ If you are **sceptical** about something, you have doubts about it. • *Other archaeologists are sceptical about his findings.*

Unit 17

confident ADJ If a person or their manner is **confident**, they feel sure about their own abilities, qualities, or ideas. • *In time he became more confident and relaxed.*

hesitant ADJ If you are **hesitant** about doing something, you do not do it quickly or immediately, usually because you are uncertain, embarrassed, or worried. • *She was hesitant about coming forward with her story.*

optimistic ADJ Someone who is **optimistic** is hopeful about the future or the success of something in particular. • *The President says she is optimistic that an agreement can be worked out soon.*

outcome N-COUNT The **outcome** of an activity, process, or situation is the situation that exists at the end of it. • *Mr. Singh said he was pleased with the outcome.*

pessimistic ADJ Someone who is **pessimistic** thinks that bad things are going to happen. • *Not everyone is so pessimistic about the future.*

Unit 19

annoyance N-UNCOUNT **Annoyance** is the feeling that you get when someone makes you feel fairly angry or impatient. • *To her annoyance the stranger did not go away.*

outrageous ADJ If you describe something as **outrageous**, you are emphasizing that it is unacceptable or very shocking. • *I must apologize for my outrageous behaviour.*

Unit 20

ironic ADJ When you make an **ironic** remark, you say something that you do not mean, as a joke. • *People used to call me Mr Popularity at high school, but they were being ironic.*

plain-speaking ADJ If you describe language as **plain-speaking,** you mean that it is clear and simple. • *The information is presented in a plain-speaking style.*

sarcasm NOUN **Sarcasm** is speech or writing which actually means the opposite of what it seems to say. Sarcasm is usually intended to mock or insult someone. • *'What a pity,' Graham said with a hint of sarcasm.*

ANSWER KEY

Unit 1   Bumping into people

Understanding

1

1 People that don't know each other well: Conversation 3

2 People that know each other well but don't see each other often: Conversation 1

3 People that see each other often: Conversation 2

2

a Asking/Checking someone's name:

It's ..., isn't it?

b Catching up with news and making small talk:

How have you been?

How did that go?

Oh, no major news really.

How are you?

What are you up to?

Where are you off to?

Same old same old.

c Inviting someone:

We should go for a coffee sometime.

Do you fancy (getting some lunch)?

d Responding to an invitation:

Definitely. Give me a ring.

Sorry, can't stop.

e Ending the conversation:

You'd better get off then.

Listen, nice to see you again but I'd better be off.

See you around.

3

1 Beth says: 'We should go for a coffee sometime'. Sometimes people say this when it isn't a real invitation but just a polite phrase.

2 With friends, it isn't always necessary to give an answer when they ask: 'How are you?'.

3 Yana has forgotten Karl's name. You can say 'Er ...?' in a questioning way to encourage someone to say their name. If that doesn't work, you will have to ask directly: 'Sorry, I can't remember your name.' or 'I recognize your face but I'm terrible with names, sorry.'

Saying it accurately

1

1 terrible with

2 better be off

3 are you up to

4 fancy going for

5 can't stop

6 are you off to

7 get off then

8 fancy seeing you

9 time no see

10 major news

Saying it appropriately

1

You is stressed to shift the focus to the other person.

2

Stressing *you* might mean the speaker has talked about themselves a lot so is trying to shift the focus to the other person.

Stressing *are* and *been* shows genuine interest as if the speaker has not seen the person for a long time and is happily surprised to be catching up.

4

1 a annoyed

2 a sincere

3 c sincere

4 a uninterested

5 b depressed

6 c interested

Everyday language

1

1 e   2 a   3 c   4 b   5 d

Unit 2   Talking about yourself

Understanding

a Talking about your strengths:

I work well in high pressure situations.

I've been told that I'm particularly good at …

I take a lot of pride in …

b Talking about your weaknesses:

I'm hopeless at …

… isn't really my strong point.

c Talking about yourself in general:

I'm (not) the kind of person who …

I wouldn't say that I …

I tend to …

I'm a bit of a …

d Talking about your experience:

I've got a background in …

When I've been in that situation in the past, I've …

e Talking about things you like:

I'm really into …

I can't get enough of it.

Saying it accurately

1

1   kind of person who   5   high pressure
2   background in   6   that situation
3   told that   7   tend, strong point
4   lot of pride

2

a

What would you say are your weaknesses? 7

b

How do you think your experience will help you in this job? 2, 3, 5

c

What do you see as your strengths? 3, 4, 5

d

Tell me a little bit about yourself. 1, 7

e

Tell me about a time when you had to deal with a difficult customer. 6

3

2   really into it   4   get enough of it
3   tend to

Saying it appropriately

1

Mick (1) and Laura (3) pause in several places because they don't know what to say. Stefan (2) and Mika (4) use slight pauses before 'I think' and 'in sales' for effect and to sound confident and capable. Stefan and Mika use stress to sound confident. Stefan stresses *Well* and *leader* to draw attention to these words and emphasize that he's a good leader. Mika stresses *sales* to emphasize that she's got a lot of extra experience that she's not mentioning.

Everyday language

Conversation 2

You must be joking!

Underneath it all …

Conversation 3

Since when do you …?

You'll think twice about …

Seriously though.

Unit 3   Telephone and communication problems

Understanding

1

Describing a problem with technology:

1   I'm getting a delay.
2   You're breaking up.
3   You keep coming and going.
4   My connection went.
5   We got cut off.
6   The reception here's terrible.
7   My battery's low.

Saying you didn't hear what someone said:

1   I didn't get most of what you just said.
2   I didn't hear a word of that!
3   I didn't catch …

Asking someone else if they heard something:

1   What are they saying?
2   Did you get that?

Saying it accurately

1

1 getting	4 low	7 saying
2 breaking	5 cut	
3 coming; going	6 went	

2

1   hold   2   have

Saying it appropriately

3

1 a	3 b	5 b	7 a	9 b
2 a	4 a	6 a	8 b	

Everyday language

1

Conversation 1	Conversation 3
Loud and clear	Are you there?

Conversation 2

at my end

Unit 4   Exchanging information

Understanding

1

a Asking for information:

I've got a couple of questions.
Can you shed some light on …?
I don't suppose you know …?
Have you got any idea …?
Can you give me any idea …?
And then what?

b Checking information:

I take it …
So you're saying …
Can you run that by me again?

c Reacting to information:

I've had a chance to go through …
I'll need some time to digest …
That's very helpful.
Okay, I get it now, I think.

2

1   Mark   2   Mark   3   a

Saying it accurately

1

1 get it	3 digest	5 run
2 go through	4 some light	

2

1   e   2   b   3   c   4   f   5   d   6   a

Saying it appropriately

1

1   b   2   a   3   a   4   b

2

Speakers a sound impatient.

3

1   any   2   then

Everyday language

1

Conversation 1

… when the time comes.

Conversation 2

There's always …

If you need any help with … just let me know.

Conversation 3

on the spot

Unit 5   Negotiating

Understanding

1 and 2

Opening a negotiation:

1   What could you come down to? T

2   You'd be looking at about … T

3   Is that a fixed price? T

4   What's the best price you can do it for? F

Making an offer or a suggestion:

1   I might be willing to drop the price by … T

2   What if …T

3   How about if we …? T

4   We should both chip in for … F

5   Will you meet me in the middle? F

Rejecting an offer:

1   The price is higher than I was looking to pay. F

2   That seems like a lot. T

Accepting an offer:

1   Okay, go on then. F

2   You've got a deal. F

3   Okay, done. F

3

In general, control of each conversation changes when someone uses one of the phrases to make an offer or reject an offer.

* marked below in red

Conversation 1

Jim: Well, I'm definitely interested but * **the price is higher than I was looking to pay** …

Seller: *__What did you have in mind?__

Jim: *Well, **what could you come down to**?

Jim: *I saw one on another stall that was a couple of hundred less, so maybe …

Seller: Well, *I **might be willing to drop the price** by a hundred.

Jim: *Knock off a hundred and fifty and I'll take it.

Conversation 2

Lana: *How do you want to organize the bills?

Eva: Well, the TV and phone package is about the same as the water bill so *__what if__ you take one and I take the other? We'll be quits then.

Lana: *__How about if we__ get a separate bank account just for bills?

Eva: Yeah, good idea! *While we're on the subject, what about household stuff? You know, washing up liquid and bits and bobs like that. *I think **we should both chip in** for that stuff.

Conversation 3

Clive: Hi, *I'm calling about some work I'm thinking of getting done.

Builder: *__You'd be looking at about__ £250 depending on what finish we give the wood.

Clive: Ah, right. Er …**That seems like a lot.** It's only a small job. *__Is that a fixed price?__

Builder: Let's see … *£230.

Clive: *I was thinking more like £180.

Builder: Huh! *The materials alone would cost me that.

Clive: *__Will you meet me in the middle?__

Saying it accurately

1

1 e	3 i	5 a	7 c	9 g
2 h	4 d	6 f	8 b	

2

1 to	3 down	5 in
2 in	4 by	6 about

Saying it appropriately

1

1 Seller: What price did <u>you</u> have in mind?

2 Tina: How about if <u>you</u> do the bathroom?

3

Speakers of sentences 1 and 4 sound the most tentative.

Everyday language

1

Conversation 2

We'll be quits.

While we're on the subject …

bits and bobs

Conversation 3

like I said, …

I was thinking more like…

Unit 6   Interrupting and letting others speak

Understanding

1

1   Mal, Regan and Heidi

2   Not at first, but they did when Mal, Regan and Heidi tried to speak more assertively and clearly.

2

a Making yourself heard:

Sorry, can I say something?

If I can get a word in edgewise

Can I just ask a question?

b Making your point:

I was just wondering…

I just wanted to say …

c Letting someone speak:

Sorry, what were you saying?

Go on.

Go ahead

Sorry, got carried away there.

After you, sorry.

No, no, after you.

3

1 c	2 d	3 b	4 a

Saying it accurately

1

1 on/ahead	3 After	5 after
2 away	4 ahead/on	

Saying it appropriately

1

The intonation is rising.

3

1 c	2 b

Everyday language

1

Conversation 1

only … weeks to go

Conversation 2

How … of us!

Conversation 3

Which brings us to …

We can't argue with …

to and from …

in the meantime

Unit 7   Showing interest

Understanding

1

a Asking questions:

Wasn't there some kind of keeper or someone?

Did you get them back?

Are you? Why's that?

Thoughtful?

b Echoing by repeating:

15 hours

Suburbs or city centre.

A list.

Disconnecting from work.

Thoughtful?

c Using synonyms:

Exhausting!

Hundreds, yeah …

… flowers!

Red and purple.

2

Exhausting!

Yeah.

Of course.

How cute!

No way!

Ah, right!

Oh, flowers!

How lovely!

3

Possible answers

1   Expressing surprise:

No way!

I don't believe it!

You're kidding!

That's unbelievable!

2   Expressing approval:

How cute!

How lovely!

Fantastic!

Wow!

That's brilliant news!

3   Expressing sympathy:

Yeah.

Oh, shame.

4   Expressing agreement:

Of course.

Absolutely.

5   Expressing understanding:

Ah, right.

Ah, I get it now.

Saying it accurately

1

1   Have you?   2   Am I?   3   Has he?

2

1   Perfect! / Your village? / Your old school?

2   We'll see! / Really high grades / You're doing okay!

3   Every day? / Good value / When you know

Saying it appropriately

1

1	a	uninterested	b	interested
2	a	interested	b	uninterested
3	a	uninterested	b	interested
4	a	interested	b	uninterested

2

1a and 2b sound sincere.

4

1   Fantastic! / Wow!   3   Absolutely.

2   You're kidding! / I don't believe it!   4   Oh, shame. / I don't believe it! / You're kidding!

Everyday language

1

1   b   3   b

2   a   4   b

Unit 8 Being supportive

Understanding

1

Finding out if someone's okay:

1 Is something wrong?
2 Are you okay?
3 You don't seem your usual self.

Expressing sympathy:

1 Everyone feels like that sometimes.
2 Sorry to hear that.
3 It's a nightmare.

Being positive:

1 Maybe it's not as bad as you think.
2 Something's bound to work out sooner or later.
3 You'll feel much better then!
4 Look on the bright side.
5 I'm sure it'll all get sorted out in the end.

Giving advice:

1 Do something to take your mind off it.
2 Maybe … would set your mind at rest.
3 Try and put it out of your mind.

Saying it accurately

1

1	e	3	a	5	d	7	b
2	g	4	c	6	f		

2

1 off   2 on   3 out

4 at   5 in   6 out

Saying it appropriately

1

1 You don't seem your usual <u>self</u>.
2 <u>Sorry</u> to hear that.
3 I'm sure it'll <u>all</u> get <u>sorted</u> out in the <u>end</u>.
4 Something's <u>bound</u> to work out <u>sooner</u> or later.
5 Maybe it's not as <u>bad</u> as you <u>think</u>.
6 Do something to take your <u>mind</u> off it.
7 Look on the <u>bright</u> side.
8 <u>Try</u> and put it <u>out</u> of your <u>mind</u>.
9 <u>Maybe</u> speaking to a <u>doctor</u> would set your <u>mind</u> at rest.

3

1 a   2 b   3 b

Everyday language

1

Conversation 1

as long as my arm

Conversation 2

I know it sounds stupid but …
It's just crept up on me.

Conversation 3

I'm flat out with …
I've barely had a minute to myself for weeks.

Unit 9 Persuasion

Understanding

1

1 Maggie and Brenda
2 Something they think they shouldn't

2

a Persuading someone to do something:

How do you know if you've never tried?
You have to admit …

Will you at least think about it?
Oh, go on!
You might not get the chance again.
One … won't hurt, will it?
You know you want to.
It makes more sense to …
Wouldn't it be easier to …?

b Being persuaded happily:

I suppose it can't hurt …

You've twisted my arm.

c Being persuaded reluctantly:

Have it your own way.

It doesn't sound like I've got much choice!

d Refusing to be persuaded:

It's not really my thing.

There's no point trying to talk me into it.

I really shouldn't …

Saying it accurately

1

1	a	3	b	5	b
2	a	4	a	6	d

2

1	twist	5	know	9	point
2	tempt	6	on	10	for
3	want	7	way		
4	off	8	thing		

Saying it appropriately

1

1   Will you at <u>least</u> think about it?

2   Will you at least <u>think</u> about it?

The first speaker sounds annoyed; the second speaker just sounds persuasive.

3

The first speaker sounds persuasive; the second speaker has been persuaded and is giving in.

Everyday language

1

Conversation 1

… as always

Conversation 2

I'm such a pushover!

Conversation 3

I see you eyeing up my …

Conversation 4

That's settled then!

Unit 10   Being tactful

Understanding

1

Downplaying negative qualities:

1   It's not that burnt.

2   Maybe it's a tad salty though.

3   I wouldn't say … exactly, but …, let's say.

4   It's nothing major.

5   … need(s) a bit more work.

6   … not quite right.

Emphasizing positive qualities:

1   It smells lovely but …

2   It's got an interesting flavour.

3   Not bad for a first attempt!

4   There are plenty of positive things …

Giving your opinion in an indirect way:

1   I'm not sure it's your colour.

2   It's not quite the right style for you.

3   It's not that. I just think …

4   He's just not exactly who …

Avoiding giving an opinion:

1   It's really none of my business.

Saying it accurately

1

1	first attempt	5	a bit / a tad
2	let's say	6	a tad / a bit
3	my business	7	not exactly
4	quite the right	8	plenty of

Saying it appropriately

1   Possible answers

1   I'm not sure it's your colour.

It's not that, I just think pink would suit you better.

It's not quite the right style for you.

2   Maybe it's a tad salty. It's got an interesting flavour.

3   Not bad for a first attempt.

4   It's really none of my business. He's just not exactly who I thought you'd end up with.

5   He's a bit direct. I wouldn't say rude exactly but he's quite forceful, let's say.

6   It needs a bit more work. This bit's not quite right.

2   Possible answers

1   It's not exactly the colour I'd choose / the colour I thought you'd choose / subtle!

2   He's just not exactly who I thought we'd end up with / who I'd choose / the best player on the team.

3   I'm not sure it's the right style for you / it's your colour.

4   It's really none of my business.

5   There are a lot of positive things in it. Maybe it needs a bit more work.

Everyday language

1

Conversation 2

slaving in the kitchen

I'm trying to watch the old waistline.

Conversation 3

You're not the first person to say that.

Conversation 4

I can feel a 'but' coming.

Such as?

Unit 11   Admitting and denying

Understanding

1

a   Chong, Leila

b   Chong, Leila, Keira

c   Elise, Derek

2

a Admitting:

I should just own up.

come clean

I hold my hands up.

b Making excuses:

I'd never have … if I'd known.

In my defence, …

I'm not trying to get out of it, but …

It's not how it looks!

I can explain!

the thing is …

I was just …

c Denying and blaming someone else:

Don't look at me!

I wasn't the last one …

It's not all my fault.

I'm not the one who …

Saying it accurately

1

1	fault	5	out of
2	defence	6	thing
3	clean	7	hold
4	own	8	look

Saying it appropriately

1

1   It's not <u>my</u> fault we're lost!

2   <u>I</u> wasn't the last one to use the oven!

3

Sentences 2, 4 and 6 are more confrontational.

4

1   b (a is too confrontational.)

2   a (b doesn't make sense because you need to deny something, not make an excuse.)

3   a (b is too confrontational.)

Everyday language

1

Conversation 1

How many times do I have to …?

Conversation 2

Wish me luck!

Conversation 3

I haven't got a clue about …

Unit 12   Gossiping

Understanding

1

1   Yolanda and Mattias; Liam is more concerned than surprised.
2   Sian
3   1 and 2
4   Germain

2

a Sharing news:

Have you heard about …?

Apparently, …

You'll never guess what I heard!

Guess what!

b Sharing a secret:

I'm not one to gossip but …

Between you and me, …

Don't tell anyone but …

c Reacting to news:

I'd never have expected that.

(She)'s the last person I'd have expected to …

3

1   b Sharing a secret
2   b Sharing a secret
3   c Reacting to news

4

Oh!

Really?

Wow!

Huh!

You're joking!

That's crazy!

Saying it accurately

1

1	Apparently	6	heard
2	gossip	7	expected
3	tell	8	never guess
4	Promise	9	anything
5	Between	10	last

Saying it appropriately

1

1   Speaker b
2   Speaker a

2

Speaker a

Everyday language

1

Conversation 2

They've only known each other five minutes.

Conversation 3

Too right!

Conversation 4

That's a major change of tune.

Unit 13   Handling difficult conversations

Understanding

1

1   b   2   a   3   c

2

a Avoiding giving an answer:

I'd rather not say, actually.

If you don't mind … I'd really rather not discuss it.

b Changing the subject:

Let's change the subject, shall we?

Okay then.

Let's just drop it, shall we?

Fine.

Anyway, …

c Expressing disapproval:

I think that's a bit harsh!

That's really out of order.

Everyone's entitled to their own opinion.

I'd rather you didn't speak to me like that.

Saying it accurately

1

1 d   2 c   3 a   4 b

Saying it appropriately

1

1 'Okay' and 'right'

2 'Anyway'

3 After 'Okay then'; after 'Anyway'

3

Speakers 2 and 4 sound firm.

5

1 a   2 b

Everyday language

1

Conversation 1

Take …, for example.

Spill the beans!

Conversation 2

in my day

How would you like it if …

Conversation 3

… wouldn't go amiss!

Unit 14   Talking about money

Understanding

1

1 Kylie and Trevor   2 Deepak

3 Mario

2

Not having enough money:

1 I can't live off that!

2 barely making ends meet

3 Money's a bit tight.

4 up to my eyes in debt

Having enough or a lot of money:

1 feeling quite flush

2 loaded

3 rolling in it

4 doing alright for (yourself)

Talking about spending money:

1 to fork out for …

2 … cost(s) me a fortune.

Offering to pay:

1 This one's on me.   3 I owe you for …

2 I'll get this.

Saying it accurately

1

1 get this	4 tight	7 rolling
2 forking out	5 flush	8 ends meet
3 eyes	6 live off	

Saying it appropriately

1

1 I'm up to my <u>eyes</u> in debt.

2 I'm <u>barely</u> making ends meet.

3 I'm <u>rolling</u> in it!

4 That holiday cost me a <u>fortune</u>!

3

1 b	3 b	5 a
2 a	4 b	

Everyday language

1

Conversation 2

Surely no one's going to …

There's no way …

The thing that gets me is …

Conversation 3

Times are tough.

Unit 15   Talking about stress

Understanding

1

1	f	3	g	5	h	7	j	9	a
2	i	4	c	6	e	8	b	10	d

2

1   help

2   been, there

3   out, bed, wrong

4   Happens, all

3

1   Someone got out of bed on the wrong side.

2   I'll snap out of it by tomorrow.

3   What is it with me and … today?

Saying it accurately

1

1   out of

2   on top of

3   over

4   under

7   snap

8   mood

9   day

10   there

Saying it appropriately

1

The first speakers (a) sound the most stressed.

2

1

It's just been <u>one thing</u> after another.

2

I'm <u>not</u> in the mood for dealing with this today!

Everyday language

1

Conversation 2

I can leave it to one side for you.

Conversation 3

to be honest

Just pop over for a while.

Conversation 4

at the minute

I'll figure it out.

Unit 16   Showing that you're sceptical

Understanding

1

1

That doesn't make much sense.

That argument doesn't hold water.

That's hardly likely to happen, is it?

There's no chance of …

I wouldn't put money on it.

I'm not buying it.

That doesn't prove anything.

2

I don't see how it follows that …

I'm not convinced.

3

Is there any evidence to back that up?

How can you be so sure?

Where's the proof?

What makes you think that?

Are you sure that's right?

2

1	b	3	b
2	a	4	a

Saying it accurately

1

1 That doesn't make much sense.
2 That's hardly likely to happen, is it?
3 I wouldn't put money on it.
4 Is there any evidence to back that up?
5 That argument doesn't hold water.
6 There could be any number of reasons for that!

2

1	chance	4	follows
2	buying	5	proof
3	convinced	6	sure

Saying it appropriately

1

1 a   2 b   3 a

2

The second speakers in conversations b sound sceptical.

Everyday language

1

Conversation 1

It was something to do with …

Conversation 2

Just you wait.

Conversation 3

You'll see.

Conversation 4

Something's going on.

Unit 17 Sounding confident or hesitant

Understanding

1

1 Sam and Richard
2 Henry
3 Sam, Liam (and Richard about Henry's presentation)
4 Cristina

2

Confident about ability:

1 All in a day's work.
2 I can … in my sleep.
3 a piece of cake
4 I'm a whizz with …

Hesitant about ability:

1 I'm not exactly an expert at …
2 It's not … that worries me, it's …
3 I'm not brilliant with …
4 It's all a bit beyond me.

Optimistic or pessimistic about a future outcome:

1 You've got it in the bag!
2 It's not looking good.
3 I can't see it happening.
4 You're bound to …

3

Confident about ability: phrases 1, 4 and 5

Hesitant about ability: phrase 3

Optimistic or pessimistic about a future outcome: phrase 2

Saying it accurately

1

1	c – C	3	f – C	5	a – H
2	b – A	4	d – H	6	e – A

2

1	whizz	5	looking
2	walk	6	bound
3	standing	7	bag
4	expert		

Saying it appropriately

1

1   b (a is too arrogant and c gives the impression of incompetence.)

2   b (a and c are insensitive and untrue in this case)

3   b or c (a sounds as if you think you'll lose)

2

1   The second speaker sounds hesitant.

2   The second speaker sounds confident.

Everyday language

1

Conversation 1

Way to go!

Conversation 2

Good for you!

... is much more up your street.

Conversation 3

You know ... inside out.

Unit 18   Sounding excited

Understanding

1

Sounding excited about something that's happening now:

1   I can't believe it.

2   I'm still pinching myself.

3   It hasn't really sunk in yet.

4   I'm thrilled to bits.

Sounding excited about something that's happening in the future:

1   I wish ... would hurry up and ...

2   I can't wait to tell ...

3   I'm really looking forward to ...

4   ... dying to ...

Sounding excited for someone else:

1   Congratulations! That's the best news ever!

2   I'm so excited for you!

3   You must be over the moon!

4   I couldn't be happier for you!

Saying it accurately

1

1	c	4	d	7	b
2	i	5	e	8	f
3	h	6	a	9	g

2

1	myself	3	it	5	You
2	you	4	you	6	it/that

Saying it appropriately

1

1, 3 and 4 sound excited; 2, 5 and 6 sound unexcited.

3

1   You must be thrilled to bits. You must be pinching yourself.

2   I'm really looking forward to it. I can't wait to go!

3   I'm over the moon! I'm thrilled to bits.

Everyday language

1

Conversation 1

All those ... really paid off.

Conversation 3

a change of scenery

It's about time!

the whole ... thing

Conversation 4

a real live ...

Unit 19   Showing annoyance and anger

Understanding

1

1	Charlotte	3	Corey
2	Hugh	4	Bobbie

2

Just take a deep breath …

Keep your hair on!

Steady on!

Just count to ten …

3

This is absolutely outrageous!

… driving me crazy

I've had it up to here with …

Saying it accurately

1

1	thing	5	count	9	nerves
2	straw	6	bugging	10	Steady
3	up	7	breath		
4	believe	8	hair		

2

1   absolutely

2   really

3   totally

4   absolutely / completely

5   really

Saying it appropriately

1

Speakers 1, 2, and 5 are fairly calm; speakers 3, 4 and 6 are angry.

Everyday language

1

Conversation 1

It's not as if …

Conversation 3

Will you shut up about …?

Conversation 4

Look at the state of …

How are we supposed to …?

Unit 20   Using sarcasm

Understanding

1

1	d	4	g	7	e
2	c	5	a		
3	f	6	b		

Saying it accurately

1

1	suddenly, expert	3	well, must, true
2	Miss	4	very

2

1	b	2	a

3

1	b	2	b	3	a

Saying it appropriately

1

Speakers b are using a sarcastic tone.

3

1 b	2 both	3 both

Everyday language

1

Conversation 3

Did you know: …

Told you!

AUDIO SCRIPT

Unit 1   Bumping into people

Track 01

(See pages 8 and 9 for audio script.)

Track 02

(See page 10 for audio script.)

Track 03

(See page 10 for audio script.)

Track 04

1

A: I've got to go. I've got a million things to do today.

B: Yeah, right … See you around then.

2

A: Well, it was great to catch up but my car's double-parked so I'd better get back to it.

B: Yeah, right. Another time then. See you around!

3

A: Hello! Carol?

B: Hi! Sorry, I'm terrible with names … Er …

4

A: Hello! Steve, isn't it?

B: Hi. Yeah. Er … Sorry, er …

5

A: Hi! How are you?

B: Knackered! How are you?

6

A: Hey, haven't seen you for a while! How are you?

B: Stressed! Work's crazy! How are you?

Track 05

(See page 11 for audio script.)

1

Hi, there. Long time no see. How are you?

[beep]

Yeah, I'm good, So, How've you been? What are you up to these days?

[beep]

Well, it's great to see you. Have you got time for a coffee? There's a really nice coffee shop near here.

[beep]

2

Hi! I thought it was you!

[beep]

Emily Anderson. We met at Paul's party. So, how are you? What have you been up to?

[beep]

Well, it's really good to catch up with you.

[beep]

Unit 2   Talking about yourself

Track 07

(See pages 12 and 13 for audio script.)

Track 08

(See page 15 for audio script.)

Track 09

1

Tell me a little bit about yourself.

[beep]

Okay, thank you, and tell me about your most recent experience in this field.

[beep]

Right. And what would you describe as your strengths?

[beep]

What would you say your weaknesses are?

[beep]

Okay, thank you. Now can you tell me about a time when you had to deal with a difficult situation?

[beep]

2

Okay, let's do this magazine quiz. Do you see yourself as sporty?

[beep]

Okay next. What music do you like?

[beep]

Aha. And are you a sociable person?

[beep]

Yes, I'd agree with that. And lastly are you a risk taker?

[beep]

Unit 3 Telephone and communication problems

Track 10

(See pages 16 and 17 for audio script.)

Track 11

(See page 18 for audio script.)

Track 12

1   Okay, Saturday is good for me. Le-e-e-et-ttttt-t-t-s me-e-e-e-e-e-tttt-t-t-t- a-a-a-a-a …

2   So he said 'Try the green one and it … *[phone cuts off]*

3   I wanted to try that new … *[unclear]* too expensive.

4

A: That's very kind. I hope you didn't …

B: Why don't you come round …

A: … go to any trouble.

B: … come round at 6. Oh, sorry …

5   *[muffled]* … the train on platform 5 will be departing 15 minutes later than scheduled.

6   So I was saying that it would be great to *[low battery beeps]* go over there later.

7   So, what do you fancy doing later? *[sound of call ending]* Argh, not again!

8   *[interference]* Hang on a minute, I think I'd better go outside …

9   *[normal volume]* As soon as *[too quiet]* you get home *[normal volume]* give me *[quiet]* a call.

Track 13

1   Would passengers for Flight A31 to Athens make their way to Boarding Gate number 14. Your flight is 45 minutes delayed due to staff shortages.

  [beep]

2   It would be great to see you. I was thinking we could meet at *[unclear: twelve by the clock]* tower and then go for lunch. But I need to be *[unclear: back at work]* by two.

  [beep]

3   **Colleague:** So, I'm calling about the monthly report. I've just seen your email. That r-r-r-r-re-eee-e-e-p-port i-i-i-i-i-i-s …

  [beep]

4   **Woman:** Hi. Where are you? I've been trying to get hold of you. I really need to talk to you. Is now a good time?

  [beep]

5   **Man:** Sorry, what did you say? I can't hear you at all … . I can't hear you …

[beep]

6   **Man:** Hello. Is that you? What happened there?

[beep]

Unit 4   Exchanging information

> **Track 14**

(See pages 20 and 21 for audio script.)

> **Track 15**

(See page 23 for audio script.)

> **Track 16**

1

So, everything okay?

[beep]

No problem, ask me anything you need to.

[beep]

Two to four weeks but it varies according to destination.

[beep]

Yes, we'll be able to advise you after you place each order.

[beep]

2

Good morning. Can I help you?

[beep]

It depends what you're interested in. There are some good art galleries near here too. And it also depends whether you mind paying to get in or not.

[beep]

Yes, some are free but to be honest the better ones charge a fee. I've got leaflets for two good ones a few minutes' walk from here.

[beep]

A friend of mine told me there's a special 1960s exhibition on at this one here, but that's all I know I'm afraid.

[beep]

Unit 5   Negotiating

> **Track 17**

(See pages 24 and 25 for audio script.)

Track 18

(See page 26 for audio script.)

Track 19

1

A: How long do you think the project will take?

B: You'd be looking at about ... two ... to ... three months.

2

A: How long do you think the project will take?

B: You'd be looking at about two to three months.

3   The price is higher than I was looking to pay.

4   The price is higher than I was looking to pay.

Track 20

1

[beep]

What did you have in mind?

[beep]

Well, you've got to remember it's in very good condition.

[beep]

I suppose I could drop the price by a hundred.

[beep]

Okay, you've got a deal.

2

What are we going to do about bills and stuff?

[beep]

So there's a double and single room, right? How do we decide who gets the double?

[beep]

Or we could just switch every six months?

[beep]

Unit 6   Interrupting and letting others speak

Track 21

(See pages 28 and 29 for audio script.)

Track 22

(See page 30 for audio script.)

1

... So, I said 'Fine if you think so, then I think so too'. But, I mean, of *course* I didn't agree! Who would? But it was easier to just go along with the decision otherwise the meeting would have gone on all morning. And we'd already had three meetings about it and no decisions reached. Hopefully we can get started on the project now because time's running out ...

2

This wing and the next wing were added in the eighteenth century ... you can see the line where the tiles are less faded, there see? Then over here we have the oldest part of the palace. It was built in the seventeenth century. It was the most expensive building of its day and visitors from other countries would come just to marvel at the stained glass and ornate ceilings. In fact, in France, there are several parts of Louis the fourteenth's ...

Track 24

1

[beep]

Sorry, can I ask a question?

[beep]

2

[beep]

Sorry, can I say something?

[beep]

3

[beep]

If I can get a word in edgeways ...

[beep]

Unit 7   Showing interest

Track 25

(See pages 32 and 33 for audio script.)

Track 26

1 a and b

A: I've just started a course in computer programming.

B: Really?

2 a and b

A: We're getting married in June and then the honeymoon's in Fiji.

B: Fiji, very nice!

3 a and b

A: I'm really not happy with the way they decorated the bedroom.

B: Aren't you?

4 a and b

A: I've got my car booked in for a service finally!

B: Oh, where?

Track 27

1 a and b

A: I'm so busy and I've had so many replies to my ad I haven't had time to respond to them all.

B: You're really busy.

2 a and b

A: I'm thinking about making a cake and some biscuits for the picnic.

B: Good idea!

Track 28

(See page 34 for audio script.)

Track 29

1   The hotel has this amazing sea view and then the mountains on the other side. It was gorgeous! And it was only $50 a night.

   [beep]

2   The food was awful and the waiter was so rude. And he overcharged us!

   [beep]

3   I've got a choice—the management job at another company or the one here that's better pay but the same level.

   [beep]

4   I love all those classic black and white films like *Casablanca* and *Breakfast at Tiffany's*.

   [beep]

5   We wanted to go and see my parents in Melbourne this weekend, but we'll have to cancel now Wendy's sick.

   [beep]

Unit 8   Being supportive

Track 30

(See pages 36 and 37 for audio script.)

Track 31

(See page 38 for audio script.)

Track 32

1

[beep]

That flat I was trying to buy has been taken off the market.

[beep]

I don't know what to do now. I have to move out of my flat at the end of this month.

[beep]

2

[beep]

My grandma's still in hospital and we don't know how long she'll be there. Test results came back okay though at least.

[beep]

Yeah, thanks. You're probably right. It's hard to concentrate on anything at the moment though. And I've got so much to do.

[beep]

Unit 9   Persuasion

Track 33

(See pages 40 and 41 for audio script.)

Track 34

(See page 42 for audio script.)

Track 35

(See page 42 for audio script.)

Track 36

1

[beep]

Sorry, I can't. I've got so much work to do for tomorrow.

[beep]

W-e-e-ll … maybe …

[beep]

I suppose it can't hurt to take a few hours off.

[beep]

2

[beep]

I'm not really that keen on the idea of being cold. I'd rather go somewhere hot.

[beep]

It's not really my thing, thanks. I like the beach!

[beep]

Well, I suppose I could look at the website.

3 and 4

Shall we have another coffee? It's really nice here, isn't it?

[beep]

Well, one more won't hurt then, will it?

[beep]

Go on, you know you want to.

[beep]

Unit 10   Being tactful

Track 37

(See pages 44 and 45 for audio script.)

Track 38

1

Do you like my bag? I made it myself from an old pair of jeans!

[beep]

It took me ages to get the top part right.

[beep]

I could make you one if you like!

[beep]

Oh, okay.

2

Here we go, my mother's recipe!

[beep]

Help yourself! Do you like it?

[beep]

3

What do you think of the new girl in our team?

[beep]

What do you mean?

[beep]

Yeah, I'm not that sure about her either!

4

Did you get a chance to go through my report?

[beep]

Oh great. So you think it's okay then?

[beep]

Unit 11   Admitting and denying

Track 39

(See pages 48 and 49 for audio script.)

Track 40

(See page 50 for audio script.)

Track 41

1, 2 and 3 Oh no! What a pain! Everything's gone. How on Earth did that happen?

[beep]

4, 5 and 6 No meat? That's the most important bit! How can we have a barbecue with no meat?

[beep]

7 Ah, hi there. Having a long lunch are you?

[beep]

Unit 12 Gossiping

Track 42

(See pages 52 and 53 for audio script.)

Track 43

(See page 55 for audio script)

Track 44

(See page 55 for audio script)

Track 45

1

[beep]

What? No way! Why would she want to do that?

[beep]

Well, good luck to her then!

2

[beep]

You're joking! He was doing so well last year! How did that happen?

[beep]

Ah. I bet his parents are furious!

[beep]

Too right! He'll work much harder when he's paying for it himself.

3

Did you hear about Annie and Carl?

[beep]

You know she's pregnant again, right? Well, they're having triplets this time!

[beep]

4

So, he goes, 'I can't give you a pay rise this year.' And I'm like, 'Er … that's not what you said in January!'

[beep]

So then he said he was freezing everyone's salaries. But I happen to know he got a big bonus this year.

[beep]

Unit 13   Handling difficult conversations

Track 46

(See pages 56 and 57 for audio script.)

Track 47

a

A: I'm going to complain. The service here is terrible!

B: Okay then … . What are we doing after this?

b

A: It's the parents I blame! It wasn't like this in my day!

B: Right. Anyway, … . Have you seen the new timetable?

Track 48

(See page 58 for audio script.)

Track 49

1

a   I heard you had loads of time off work recently. Sick were you? What was wrong?

[beep]

b   What an idiot your boss is! I can't believe they made him our team leader too!

[beep]

c   Didn't anyone teach you how to use a photocopier! Honestly, how did you ever get the job?

[beep]

2

a   Your sister's got some very strange ideas, that's all I'm going to say! What was she thinking decorating the whole house in pink, though?

[beep]

b   It's a question of class and taste. Some people have it, some don't. And your friend Laurence certainly doesn't have either!

[beep]

c   Ugh, please save me from people with children! All they ever want to talk about is nappies and school plays!

[beep]

Unit 14   Talking about money

Track 50

(See pages 60 and 61 for audio script.)

Track 51

(See page 62 for audio script.)

Track 52

1   Hey, I'm selling my car. You interested in buying it?

[beep]

2   Do you want to go out for a drink tonight?

[beep]

3   Do you want to come skiing with us in France at Christmas? It's a five-star hotel and we need to rent all the gear and pay for the flights.

[beep]

4   Shall we try that new café for lunch?

[beep]

5   If you want to replace your laptop with the top-of-the-range technology, we've got the latest Mac™ in store.

[beep]

Track 53

Don't worry. I'll get this.

[beep]

No, no, let me.

[beep]

Oh well, okay, then. Thanks a lot! That's very kind of you.

Unit 15   Talking about stress

Track 54

(See pages 64 and 65 for audio script.)

Track 55

(See page 66 for audio script.)

Track 56

1

What's happened to you this morning?

[beep]

Woah, someone got out of bed on the wrong side!

[beep]

2

Hey? Is something wrong?

[beep]

Happens to us all. Don't worry about it.

[beep]

3

You okay? What happened?

[beep]

Oh, we've all been there. Anything I can do to help?

[beep]

Track 57

1   Argh! This stupid computer's crashed again! What is it with me and computers today?

    [beep]

2   Oh, it's really not my day today! Everything's going wrong!

    [beep]

3   Oh, it's just been one thing after another today! It's really not my day! And now I've lost my wallet!

    [beep]

Unit 16   Showing that you're sceptical

Track 58

(See pages 68 and 69 for audio script.)

Track 59

1 a and b

A: There's no way people really walked on the moon. I read this article about how they faked the whole thing.

B: Mmmmm.

2 a

A: The Raj is easily the best curry place in this area.

B: Mmmm. Really!

b

A: The Raj is easily the best curry place in this area.

B: Mmmm. Really?

Track 60

1   I'm sure there are aliens. I've seen some strange things in the sky when I've been in the mountains.

    [beep]

2   The way technology is advancing, time travel will be within humankind's reach one day. I mean, a few hundred years ago we could never have imagined going to the moon!

   [beep]

3   I reckon we've got about 20 years left until people have destroyed the Earth. 50 years max.

   [beep]

4   Anyone can learn English – any language in fact – if they just study hard enough. Read, watch TV, study grammar. You just have to put in the effort and you'll be native-speaker level if you really want.

   [beep]

5   Of course Italian food is the best in the world! I mean, if it wasn't the best, there wouldn't be pizza restaurants all over the world, would there?

   [beep]

Unit 17   Sounding confident or hesitant

Track 61

(See pages 72 and 73 for audio script.)

Track 62

1 and 2

A: Do you know how to use this software?

B: Er … yeah … maybe. I'll give it a go.

Track 63

1

Have you seen who they've got playing? Some of those guys are regional champions.

[beep]

Maybe … but I really think we're going to struggle today.

[beep]

2

What do you think about our team today?

[beep]

Mmm, yeah. Do you think we have a chance of winning?

[beep]

3 and 4

How are you feeling about the exam this afternoon?

[beep]

I'm sure you'll do the best you can.

[beep]

Well, good luck and let me know how it goes!

Unit 18   Sounding excited

Track 64

(See pages 76 and 77 for audio script.)

Tracks 65 and 66

(See page 78 for audio script.)

Track 67

1   So, you're all booked to go on safari in Kenya? You must be so excited!
    [beep]
2   Wow! I can't believe you won £10,000 – I'm so happy for you!
    [beep]
3   I've just won a poetry-writing competition! First prize is a week's holiday in Spain!
    [beep]
4   Congratulations on passing your driving test!
    [beep]
5   I heard you got that promotion. Well done!
    [beep]
6   We did it! The record company saw me on the Internet and they've offered me a record deal!
    [beep]
7   When does term start? Are you excited about going back to university?
    [beep]

Unit 19   Showing annoyance and anger

Track 68

(See pages 80 and 81 for audio script.)

Tracks 69, 70 and 71

(See page 82 for audio script.)

Track 72

1   The A305 to Cairo has been cancelled due to adverse weather conditions. All passengers please go to the information desk for assistance.
    [beep]
2   … and there will be heavy rain and thunderstorms throughout the bank holiday weekend. You might want to rethink that picnic!
    [beep]

3   Diversion ahead. Take alternative route. Diversion ahead.

    [beep]

4   It's run out of cash. Great!

    [beep]

5   I've used all the milk again, sorry. I'll get some in the morning when the shops open.

    [beep]

Track 73

1   Argh! I don't believe it! This stupid thing! Oh, this is so annoying! Why isn't it working?

    [beep]

2   Right, I'm sick of this now! This is the last time I'm dealing with this nonsense. I'm going to go in there and tell him exactly what I think of him!

    [beep]

Unit 20   Using sarcasm

Track 74

(See pages 84 and 85 for audio script.)

Track 75

(See page 86 for audio script.)

Track 76

1   Oh, no! I think it's going to rain!

    [beep]

2   How's your burger?

    [beep]

3   [beep]

    Oh, sorry. Is it too loud?

    [beep]

4   Look! This article says everyone will be wearing red shoes this autumn. And leather's back in fashion, too.

    [beep]

ACKNOWLEDGEMENTS

Photo credits

All images are from Shutterstock.

Cover: wavebreakmedia; p8: bikeriderlondon; p12: Adam Gregor; p16: oliveromg; p20: Iakov Filimonov; p24: Monkey Business Images; p28: wavebreakmedia; p32: bikeriderlondon; p36: Monkey Business Images; p40: Goodluz; p44: Antonio Guillem; p48: Elle1; p52: Vladimir Melnikov; p56: Monkey Business Images; p60: CandyBox Images; p64: DoctorKan; p68: Sergey Furtaev; p72: Andrey_Popov; p76: Sabphoto; p80: Aaron Amat; p84: savageultralight.

Trademarks referenced in this book

Skype™

Powerpoint™ (a registered trademark of Microsoft)

Collins   Also available